Ca

Copyright ©1997 by Ruth J.F. Frey

All rights reserved. No part of this book may be reproduced in any form or by any electronic or mechanical means, including information storage and retrieval systems, without permission in writing from the publisher, except brief passages presented in a review.

BRUSH CREEK BOOKS
1317 Livingston Street
Evanston, Illinois 60201-1626
847-328-2844

Cover and illustrations by Donna Currier
Book design by Rivera Design & Communications

ISBN # 0-9636187-2-5
Library of Congress Catalog Card Number: 97-93067

Printed in the United States of America

Disclaimer
Bicycling involves potential risks. Cyclists should be aware of inherent dangers, should know and obey Colorado's rules of the road, and should understand and practice safe and courteous behavior on trails designated for cyclists, pedestrians and equestrians. While the author has made every effort to be precise and accurate, cyclists must expect that road and trail conditions may change due to weather and maintenance. Roads and trails are also subject to realignment and resurfacing. Motor vehicle traffic can be extremely variable. Brush Creek Books and the author do not warrant that the actual status of roads and trails will conform to published descriptions and maps. Brush Creek Books and the author assume no liability for injury or accident. Descriptions of these bicycling routes do not constitute an endorsement or a recommendation.

Restaurants are notorious for changing menus, hours of operation and location. Sometimes they vanish altogether. Brush Creek Books and the author assume no liability for any problems that anyone may experience at one or more of the restaurants described in this book. A description of a restaurant does not constitute an endorsement or a recommendation.

Café Cycling
Aspen to Glenwood Springs

Ruth Frey

Brush Creek Books

THANKS

*To the friends
who
at great personal sacrifice
joined me for bike rides and field trips to restaurants.
Their faithful dedication
to this arduous research
is appreciated.*

and

*To those who read portions of my manuscript,
who freely responded to my questions,
or who furnished needed documents.*

Paul Andersen, freelance writer and master mountain biker
Bud Eylar, Pitkin County Engineer
Margot Frey, sales sensation and indulgent daughter
Charles Harris, retired rancher, storekeeper and jack-of-all-trades
Paul Hilts, Director of Operations, Roaring Fork Transit Agency
A.P. "Jake" Jacobson, retired academician and tireless fisherman
Richard Kolecki, Superintendent, Glenwood Hatchery, Colorado DOW
Cathy Kulzer, Office & Project Manager, The Roaring Fork Club
John McCarty, Landscape Architect/Environmental Planner, S'mass Vllg.
Edmund Miller, Asst. Project Manager for Hwy 82 Corridor, CDOT
Gay Page, Coordinator, CDOT: Bicycle Pedestrian Program
Brent Gardner-Smith, Director of Marketing, Aspen Skiing Company
Joan Lamb Ullyot, Jungian therapist and running legend

to
PETER,
for everything

TABLE OF CONTENTS

Overview Map VIII
Key IX
Bicycle Services X
From the Author XV

Preliminaries 1
Preparation 3
Skills 10
Safety & Etiquette 17

Aspen West End Tour 23
Meadows Restaurant 28
Aspen Alfresco 31
Smuggler Mountain Grind Bonus Ride 43
East of Aspen Bonus Ride 44

Aspen to Ashcroft 45
Pine Creek Cookhouse 50

Aspen to Maroon Bells 53
Aspen Picnic Provisions 58

Snowmass Village to Aspen 59
Snowmass Patios 65
Village Fast Fare 70
Snowmass Lifts Bonus Ride 71

5 Aspen to Woody Creek 73
    Woody Creek Tavern 78

6 Woody Creek to Lenado 81

7 Woody Creek to Basalt 87
    Charcoal Kilns Sidetrip 92
    Basalt's Best 93

8 Basalt-Old Snowmass Loop 97
    St. Benedict's Monastery Sidetrip 101

9 Basalt to El Jebel 103
    Grana Bread Company Sidetrip 107
    El Jebel Portable Edibles 108

10 El Jebel to Carbondale 109
    Carbondale Cuisine 115

11 Basalt-Carbondale Loop 119

12 Glenwood Canyon 125
    Hanging Lake Hike Sidetrip 129

13 Glenwood to Fish Hatchery 131
    Glenwood Fare 136

Café Cycling Ride Summaries 145

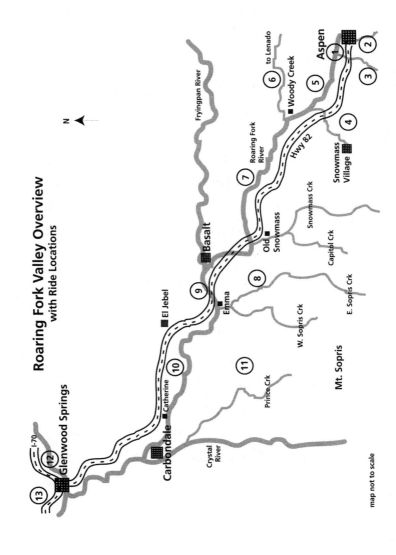

Key to Icons

Ride Level of Difficulty

 Two easy rides. Round trip of 4.8 to 10.2 miles. Maximum elevation change of 191 feet.

 Four easy/moderate rides. Round trip of 8.0 to 30.8 miles. Maximum elevation change of 480 feet.

 Two moderate rides. Round trip of 19.8 to 24.8 miles. Maximum elevation change of 776 feet.

 Five moderate/ambitious rides. Round trip of 15.0 to 29.0 miles. Maximum elevation change of 1899 feet.

Ride and Map Information

 drinking water
 restaurant, café, bakery
 bike repair, parts
 pay telephone
 picnic table
 restroom
 privy
 bike rack for lockup
 bus stop for bike-loading
(P) parking

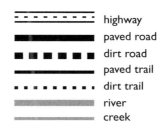

BICYCLE SERVICES

Name	Sales	Rentals	One-way	Repairs	Closed
A. Ajax Bike & Sports	b c p	h k l m r s t x	y	y	-
B. Aspen Ski Mart-Bikes	-	h m s	n	n	Sun
C. Timberline at Stefan Kaelin	c	h k l m r s t x	n	n	-
D. Christy Sports	-	h m s	y	n	-
E. Aspen Sports on Cooper Av.	c p	h k l m s t x	y	n	-
F. Aspen Sports at Ritz Carlton	c p	h k l m s t x	y	n	-
G. Hub of Aspen	b c p	h l m s t	n	y	-
H. Bicycle Service Center	b p	-	-	y	Sat. Sun
I. Aspen Velo	b c p	h k l m r s	y	y	-
J. Use It Again (resale)	b c p	h m	n	n	Sun
K. Aspen Sports at SV Center	c p	h k l m s x	y	y	-
L. Sidewinder Sports	b c p	h k m s	n	y	-
M. Gene Taylor Sports	b c p	h k l m s	n	n	-
N. D & E Snowboard Shop	b c p	h k m s	n	y	-
O. Christy Sports on SV Mall	c	h k l m s	y	n	-
P. Aspen Sports on SV Mall	c	h k l m s x	y	n	-
Q. Aspen Velo on SV Mall	c p	h k l m s	y	y	-
R. Pomeroy Sports	b c p	h k l m r s x	y	y	-
S. Ajax Bike & Sports in C'dale	b c p	m s x	y	y	-
T. Life Cycles	b c p	h k l m r s x	n	y	-
U. Ski Sunlight Ski & Bike	b c p	h k l m s	n	y	-

x

Name	Sales	Rentals	One-way	Repairs	Closed
V. Cycles Plus	p	-	n	y	M,T
W. Sunlight Sports	b c p	h k l m s x	n	y	-
X. BSR Sports	b c p	h k l m s x	n	y	Sun
Y. Canyon Bikes at Hotel Colorado	-	h k l m t x	y	n	-

Key to Services:

b = bikes	l = trailers & trail-a-bikes	s = front or dual suspension
c = clothing & accessories	m = mountain bikes	t = tandem bikes
h = helmets & locks	p = parts	x = cross/hybrid bikes
k = kid-size bikes	r = road bikes	

NOTE: Bike rental fees always cover the use of a bicycle, a helmet and, in most cases, a lock. Canyon, Christy and Timberline also include bike bags for storage of small items. For health reasons, water bottles must be purchased new or be supplied by the rider. A minimum rental period is usually two hours, and discounts are available for weekly or monthly rentals. Days "closed" pertains to summer season only.

ONE-WAY (DOWNHILL) BICYCLE RENTALS

Unidirectional rides have real appeal in the mountains. For a descent from Snowmass Village to Aspen, rent a bicycle from Aspen Sports, Aspen Velo or Christy Sports: All three businesses have outlets in both communities. Upon request, Pomeroy Sports will move bikes to its Aspen store for the glide back to its Basalt location. For a long, sweet cruise and an elevation loss of 1727 feet, rent from Ajax Bike in Aspen and cycle 30 miles to Ajax in Carbondale. The valley's bus system can return you to your start. In Glenwood Springs, Canyon Bikes will shuttle cyclists to the upper terminus of the Colorado River Trail at Dotsero, leaving them to meander downriver for 16 scenic miles.

BICYCLE SERVICES LOCATIONS

Aspen	**Address**	**Telephone**
A. Ajax Bike & Sports	635 E. Hyman Av.	925-7662
B. Aspen Ski Mart-Bikes	430 S. Spring St.	925-9169
C. Timberline at Stefan Kaelin	447 E. Cooper Av.	920-3217
D. Christy Sports	516 E. Durant St.	920-1170
E. Aspen Sports	408 E. Cooper Av.	925-6331
F. Aspen Sports at Ritz Carlton	303 E. Durant St.	925-6332
G. Hub of Aspen	315 E. Hyman Av.	925-7970
H. Bicycle Service Center	609 Rio Grande Pl.	920-9709
I. Aspen Velo	465 N. Mill St.	925-1495
J. Use It Again (resale)	465 N. Mill St.	925-2483

Snowmass Village

K. Aspen Sports	Snowmass Center	923-3566
L. Sidewinder Sports	Snowmass Mall	923-3708
M. Gene Taylor Sports	Snowmass Mall	923-4336
N. D & E Snowboard Shop	Snowmass Mall	923-2337
O. Christy Sports	Snowmass Mall	923-2717
P. Aspen Sports	Snowmass Mall	923-6111
Q. Aspen Velo	Snowmass Mall	923-5507

Basalt

R. Pomeroy Sports	132 Midland Av.	927-3760

Carbondale

S. Ajax Bike & Sports	419 Main St.	963-0128
T. Life Cycles	0902 Highway 133	963-1149

Glenwood Springs

U. Ski Sunlight Ski & Bike	1315 Grand Av.	945-9425
V. Cycles Plus	906 Cooper Av.	945-7317
W. Sunlight Sports	931 Grand Av.	945-8958
X. BSR Sports	210 7th St.	945-7317
Y. Canyon Bikes at Hotel Colorado	319 6th St.	945-8904

NOTE: Summer hours for full-service and rental-only locations are generally from 9 a.m. until 6 p.m. Some close as late as 7 or 8 p.m. Repair shops have more limited hours. If you anticipate an early start or have special needs, telephone the previous day to check opening time and availability of equipment. Ask about closing time before departing for the day. Spring and fall hours are usually abbreviated, and rental-only places may shut down completely by mid-September. As hours, services and even locations change, calling ahead is *always* a good idea.

THE BIKE-ON-BUS OPTION

Cyclists who fancy a downhill cruise to a downvalley town can avoid the return trip. Buses of the Roaring Fork Transit Agency are equipped with exterior bike racks. But this option to pumping back to Aspen or Snowmass Village has limitations. Each bus transports four bicycles only, introducing potential competition for space. Bikes may be loaded only at designated stops. And a fee is levied for each bicycle transported.

The scramble for spaces is most intense on the route to Snowmass Village from the intercept lot at Brush Creek Road and Highway 82. All Snowmass-bound riders transfer here. High demand means that a cyclist pays a passenger fare for each leg of the journey plus one bike fee for the entire trip.

As of early 1997, the following stops were designated for bicycle loading and unloading:

- Rubey Park on Durant Street in Aspen
- Aspen Airport Business Center
- Brush Creek Road intercept lot
- Snowmass Village Mall
- Aspen Village mobile home park
- Old Snowmass intersection
- Lions Park in central Basalt
- El Jebel park-and-ride lot near bowling alley
- Sopris Park in downtown Carbondale
- Wal-Mart in Glenwood Springs
- West Glenwood Mall

Modifications are possible for the bike-on-bus policy and for bus-loading locations. Call RFTA's information line at 925-8484 for updates and current fares, and ask about the printed flyer which describes the program in detail. As exact fare is required for both riders and bicycles, consider purchasing a multiride punch pass, saving both money and the hunt for change.

FROM THE AUTHOR

A Guiding Philosophy

Life tilts out of balance so easily, so subtly. Forgotten are the words of Agnes Repplier: "It is in pleasure that a man really lives; it is from his leisure that he constructs the true fabric of self." Preoccupied with responsibility, busy people often put recreation on hold. But in these mountains, where the very air bestows vitality, play seems natural, compelling.

This guide fuses sensual elements into a gratifying trio: nature, exercise and food. In this delicious mix are the beauty of this storied region, the physical elation of cycling and the culinary inventions of local chefs. Add cheerful comrades and beget a mobile celebration—a party on wheels.

While I expect to update this book periodically as cafés and trails transfigure and multiply, I pledge not to tamper with the pleasure principle, the philosophy that governs *Café Cycling*.

Café Criteria

This valley's culinary community has spawned a happy profusion of restaurants, cafés, coffeehouses, bakeries and delicatessens. Food—glorious food—is everywhere. So, how to choose?

To make this book portable, I was compelled to set criteria for inclusion of eateries. So alone, or accompanied by the gourmand or the curious, I embarked upon a rigorous campaign of cycling and eating, eating and cycling, all the while taking notes, chatting with diners, questioning restaurateurs. Without aspiring to be a food critic, I acquired preferences and saw what worked for cyclists. Even with constraints, there is bountiful choice.

Nearly all establishments profiled here deliver an alfresco dining experience in keeping with the outdoor theme of summer cycling. If there is no patio, terrace, deck or balcony, there is a special quality to the cuisine or the indoor ambiance. Food stops are situated along a biking route and are open in daytime hours when cyclists take to their wheels. All dispense breakfast, brunch, lunch, snacks or picnic fare. They possess a welcoming, come-in-your-bike-shorts attitude, and they proffer tasty food at modest to moderate prices.

Be advised that "Diner Favorites" refers to an eatery's most popular menu items–those entrées, nibbles and beverages most often ordered by patrons.

This guide, of course, will always be a work in progress. Restaurants founder and vanish, leaving diners and authors in the lurch. Revised editions will require fresh material about new or overlooked culinary treasures. Readers are urged to nominate replacements and additions by contacting Brush Creek Books, P.O. Box 5313, Snowmass Village, CO 81615.

Ride Criteria

Most of the tours in this guide qualify as recreational fun. They require no mountain biking finesse—those techniques for fording streams, for threading dense woods, for vaulting over logs, gullies and fallen companions. While exhilarating to some, there is none of that here.

Instead, the selected rides deliver wonderful scenery, easy access and familiar amenities. Natural beauty is everywhere—in roadside wildflowers and turbulent creeks and snowy peaks. Trailheads are in towns and villages, close to lodging or parking. Trips end where they start, eliminating the need for two cars or connecting bus service. Amenities—cafés, fresh water, restrooms, bike shops—are rarely far away. Such criteria eliminated some road routes and all backcountry excursions.

Ride summary information should help cyclists choose a tour. Time estimates are omitted as the focus is on leisurely enjoyment, not fitness. Start early enough to contend with a bike malfunction, and remember that riding dirt roads takes longer than riding pavement. Long ascents also slow cyclists down. Expect to rest, to sightsee, to dine and drink. Expect to have fun.

0 Preliminaries

"All around were fine mountain peaks....
No wonder, I thought, that the people of the plains
have their gods live here; no wonder, too,
that anyone seeking the world of the spirit
should travel here to find it amidst the
mysteries of snow, mountains, sky, and
clouds and high pastures."

— Sir Edmund Hillary

PREPARATION

RECIPE FOR SUCCESS

A CAFÉ CYCLING TRIP SHOULD BE FUN. And the Roaring Fork Valley has the right ingredients for a gourmet ride. But like a cook, the cyclist must read the recipe, season with good sense, and mix well. The result can be delicious.

1. Begin by helping your body to adjust to high altitude. See "Natural Hazards."

2. Read about several routes and compare distances, elevation gains and riding surfaces.

3. Assess the fitness levels and riding skills of your companions by starting with an easy ride rather than a long loop with hills and gravel.

4. Know if a bus intersects your route and have exact change, or a multi-ride punch pass, should you want to bail out of the tour.

5. Assemble the clothing, gear, energy snacks and water needed for the trip.

6. Keep breakfast light but high in carbos; a full stomach and fatty foods reduce endurance and performance.

7. Check tire pressure on your bicycle and adjust for the riding surface. Pressure should be higher for pavement than for dirt.

8. Take a test spin on a rental bike to check its size and condition. Change bikes if you are uncomfortable.

9. Start early to avoid thunderstorms or heat, and put off the ride if the weather is unstable.

10. Garnish with every oasis! Bon appétit!

Natural Hazards

Most of the tours in this guide stick close to civilization, usually traveling between towns and villages. But high altitude and volatile weather can complicate any ride. Read on for tips on comfort and safety.

Altitude

High elevation affects your body and influences the weather. It impacts every decision made in planning for a trip: route and clothing chosen, evaluation of fitness and ability, and amount and types of food and liquid consumed.

Altitudes's effects are usually felt immediately upon arriving in the mountains from the flatlands or seacoast. At first, all exercise, including stair-climbing, is harder work. Visitors often experience heavy breathing, rapid heartbeat, fatigue, headache, frequent urination, nausea, constipation or insomnia. This is normal. Your body is simply engaged in making enough hemoglobin, the oxygen-carrying component in blood, to compensate for the lower air pressure of high elevation. In Aspen, for instance, each breath takes in only 70 to 80 percent of the oxygen available at sea level.

You can minimize the effects of high altitude: Drink lots of water; avoid alcohol; eat light, high-carbohydrate meals; increase physical activity gradually; and rest when tired. Aspirin or ibuprofen can help with headaches. After about four days, most visitors feel better. Improvement continues for weeks.

Dehydration

Water loss occurs rapidly when exercising at high altitude. Low humidity, direct sun and perspiration are themselves a potent combination. But while biking, the movement of air over your body is accelerating water loss from skin and mucous membranes. If you are thirsty, dehydration has already begun.

Drink water or sports drinks before, during and after a ride. Try to consume no less than a pint of liquid per hour while exercising. Drink every 15 to 20 minutes even if the sensation of thirst is absent. Carry a large water bottle on your bike or strap on a Camelbak™ system for steady access to water through a tube.

Before setting out, check this guide's route descriptions. Icons mark all locations where water or other liquids are available. Refill your bottle and stop often to drink.

Sun

With less atmosphere to filter out the sun's harmful rays, mountain cyclists are more vulnerable to sunburn. There is five times more ultraviolet light at the Maroon Bells or Ashcroft, for instance, than at sea level. Apply sunblock lotions or wear protective clothing. The intense sunshine can produce withering heat in open areas. At midday it can sap energy, deliver headaches and contribute to dehydration. In hot weather, try to ride in the early morning or late afternoon. And drink, drink, drink to avoid heat stroke and heat exhaustion.

Rain

Rocky Mountain weather is notorious for its volatility. Sunny, summer mornings are frequently paired with afternoon showers or thunderstorms. Hail and even snow are possible. Rain presents several problems: It can chill the rider, contributing to hypothermia; and it can impair visibility, presenting dangers to cyclists sharing narrow, twisting roads with cars, trucks and bulky RVs. Dirt trails can become slippery with mud, and wet, steel railroad tracks that cross roads *at an angle* can set up a crash.

Start early. Stay loose. Adjust your plans to conditions. And always travel with a waterproof, breathable jacket, even on short rides. Rain pants and plastic bags to wear under your shoes are good insurance for longer trips.

Cold

Cool mornings are common even in midsummer. A wind-rain shell adds warmth when needed and can be removed as the day heats up. In other seasons, long sleeves, leggings and fleece are good. The real danger is cold combined with wetness and/or wind: conditions perfect for hypothermia. Hypothermia is loss of heat in the body's inner core. It affects the functioning of all bodily systems. If unchecked, hypothermia can kill.

If you are caught unprepared in a cold, wet and windy situation, seek shelter in a warm, dry place or hitch a ride home. Strip off wet clothes, drink heated liquids, eat, and sink into a warm bath.

Wind
A landscape of peaks and valleys channels wind in unpredictable ways. It often seems to be blowing from all directions. One trick is to follow the daily up-down air flow. In the early morning, air heats and moves upslope, offering a tail wind to riders; in late afternoon, the air cools, moving downslope. Deal with strong headwinds by conserving energy: Settle into an easy pace, keep a low profile on the bike, rest occasionally, and snack on sweet foods.

Lightning
Always retreat when bad weather threatens. But if caught in a lightning storm, find shelter in a place with cover, preferably in a low but *dry* spot. A stand of trees of similar heights is good. If you are in the open, crouch down, making yourself small. Distance yourself from your bicycle and all metal objects. And always avoid the company of a lone tree or boulder.

THE RIGHT BIKE

While road bikes are appropriate for many of this book's rides, mountain bikes are popular in Aspen because they can handle all terrain. Built something like our sturdy, childhood two-wheelers, mountain bikes can stand up to abuse. But unlike those one-speeds, these machines can climb and climb, thanks to anywhere from 18 to 24 speeds, lighter materials and modern engineering. If you have not ridden mountain bikes before, you will be impressed with their stability over uneven surfaces: Their low stance and fat tires enhance the feeling of control. Even timid riders should feel secure.

Bike geometry affects body position and handling, critical in "extreme" situations. But the trail and road routes in this guide are not in the extreme category and do not put excessive demands on cyclists. Select a bicycle that seems comfortable for you and that keeps you in control; you want to be master of the machine. In any case, rent before you buy.

Mountain bike frames are not built and sized like frames of streamlined touring bikes. Get yourself measured at a bike shop for the best fit. It is important that you are able to straddle the top horizontal frame tube with feet flat on the ground and a *minimum* of two inches to spare between your crotch and the bar. This clearance is required for rougher terrain. Adjust the seat so that you can sit comfortably with the leg *almost* fully extended when the pedal is in the bottom rotation position. Your knees should not lock. And a seat that is too low can deliver strain and pain to knees and back, seriously reducing the fun factor.

A real bummer is fanny fatigue. Your bottom will be less sore if your riding position distributes some weight on the balls of your feet, if you wear padded cycling shorts, and if you find a saddle that matches your contours. Women might want to check out a slightly wider and slightly shorter saddle with a cutout or indentation in the shell to reduce pressure on sensitive tissues. But be careful: A saddle that is too wide will impair movement. The good news is that soreness diminishes with regular riding.

HELMETS & SHADES

Okay, so bicycle helmets *can* look pretty dorky. Until recently, it was virtually impossible to be chic, sassy or sporting with that bowl on your belfry. Even swank shades helped precious little, although they *might* conceal your identity.

But behold today's dashing headgear. Sleek and aerodynamic, gleaming silver or regal purple, festooned with racing stripes or snazzy visors, the new helmets are de rigueur for fitness aficionados and speed freaks. You may never want to take yours off.

As a cyclist, the smartest thing you can do for yourself is to wear a helmet. If you are in an accident, you are 60 percent more likely to die if your head is unprotected. But only some helmets meet safety standards; look for ANSI or Snell certification. Be particular about a snug fit, cinch the chin straps to minimize movement, and wear the helmet in a level position, not tilted backward or at a jaunty angle. It comes down to this: What value do you place on your brain?

Think about safeguarding your eyes too. Sunglasses can protect against ultraviolet rays, insects, debris and wind. And they *always* have élan.

Good Gear

Water is the single most important item to take on a ride. Purchase a bottle specifically designed for the bicycle's attached cage, or wear a water-filled backpack equipped with a long, flexible straw, or stow away plastic bottles in a bike or body pack.

A bike bag, waist pack or daypack can hold items that should travel with you:

- rain jacket
- lip balm
- energy snacks
- bus schedule
- sunscreen
- map or guidebook
- money, including quarters for telephone
- packaged towelettes, bandaids, ibuprofen
- personal identification

As most tours in this guide follow well-traveled roads and trails, a bicycle repair kit and extensive first aid supplies are not mandatory. Road riding, however, is safer with a rearview mirror mounted on your handlebars, sunglasses or helmet. A bell warns others of your approach. Bindings—toe clips, pedal straps, clipless pedals—keep feet snug to pedals over bumps and add power on the upstroke when hill climbing, but practice is needed to get in and out of these contraptions.

Good Garb

While it is certainly possible to pedal a bicycle while wearing almost anything, today's cycling clothes really are well designed and really do contribute to riding comfort. And, well, they really do look pretty slick. The bikers pictured on page 1 model current fashions.

For short rides, almost any shirt will do. But for extended workouts, breathable fabrics are terrific as they allow wetness to evaporate. A front zipper helps regulate heat, and back pockets stow away snacks and small items.

Prolonged contact with a bike saddle generates soreness, and fabric that bunches in the crotch of pants results in nasty chafing and abrasions. Protect your bottom with stretchy, body-hugging, padded shorts. Skip the underwear: Seams and elastic edges can do real damage. If you are shy about revealing every curve, look for variations on this design: a stretchy padded layer topped by attached loose shorts; roomy shorts designed with a cushioned crotch; or snug, padded underwear worn under regular pants.

Fingerless gloves with cushioned palms make a difference on longer trips, and sport shoes work best if not too bulky. If you opt for pedal bindings, footgear must be appropriate for the type of binding.

In spring and fall, switch to a long-sleeved polypropylene jersey, cycling tights and full-fingered gloves. On really cold days, add synthetic long underwear or a fleece layer, and wear a thin knit cap under your helmet. Carry a breathable rain jacket in all seasons. And in autumn, when hunters are armed and dangerous, don brightly colored clothing for backcountry riding: fluorescent orange, bubble gum pink, tropical magenta . . . .

SKILLS

BODY BASICS

A MOUNTAIN BIKE SHOULD FEEL LIKE A POWERFUL EXTENSION of yourself. Adjust the vehicle to you and then adjust your body position to the vehicle. The right relationship can make cycling easier, more efficient and, inevitably, more fun.

1. Get measured at a bike shop to determine the best frame size for *you*.

2. Adjust the seat height so that your leg is nearly straight when the pedal is at the bottom of the rotation. See the illustration on page 7.

3. Hold handlebar grips firmly without putting weight forward on them. Have the bars raised if they seem too low.

4. Bend elbows slightly to absorb shocks from bumps and to relax arms, thus reducing fatigue from tension in arms, shoulders and back.

5. Distribute your weight between the seat and the pedals.

6. Rise slightly off the seat when riding over bumps; you will reduce saddle soreness.

7. Angle toes in slightly, keeping knees close to the top tube of the bike's frame. This leads to efficient, stronger pedaling with less stress on joints.

8. Change your body position occasionally to reduce muscle tension: Move forward or back on the saddle, or put the bike in a higher/harder gear and stand up to pedal for a short distance.

9. Use your whole body to help you on curves by leaning gently toward the inside of the curve; for a tighter turn at higher

speed, stick an elbow or knee out from the body in the direction of the turn to get more lean.

10. Dismount, stretch and breathe deeply if you find yourself tightening up.

ROLLING TERRAIN

Many tours in this guide trace the floor of the Roaring Fork Valley. These pleasant rides are made interesting by small dips and rises. Techniques for dealing with rolling terrain take a little time to learn, but with practice they lead to efficient and almost effortless cycling. Your goal is a seamless melding of uphill and downhill skills.

Understanding your bike's gears is essential. Practice with them on level ground so that you know what each change does to cadence and resistance. The bike's left gearshift controls the three front sprocket rings mounted between the pedals; moving between them makes *big* changes in resistance. The right gearshift is linked to the rear wheel's six to eight sprocket rings; moving from one to another makes *fine* adjustments. To switch smoothly from one front ring to another, one of the *middle* rear sprocket rings must be engaged.

Downshifting, or dropping to a lower gear, means easier pedaling but a slower pace; shifting up requires more force on the pedals but advances the bicycle farther with each rotation.

The real keys to fluent transitions over rolling terrain are to transfer downhill momentum to the next climb and to time gear changes to maintain steady speed and exertion.

To get a running start for the uphill ahead, lower your profile, move back on the saddle, and pedal as you approach the bottom of a grade. Position your gears before the climb by shifting to a lower front gear (a smaller sprocket ring) and by moving the chain to a higher gear (also a smaller sprocket ring) on the rear wheel. This allows you to downshift with your back derailleur multiple times before reaching the crest.

It takes some riding experience to sense the right moment to shift weight forward and to change gears as you climb. But if you feel your chain tension tightening and your pedaling becoming harder, shift to a lower gear to ease resistance on both chain and legs. Begin to downshift while you still have momentum and continue to do so when needed, always before coming to a halt. Once stopped on an upgrade, it may be difficult to change gears or start pedaling again.

If the hill is quite short, you can avoid downshifting by muscling your way to the top or standing to pedal—a power move for limited distances.

A comfortable gear combination for uphills will be inefficient for stretches of level ground. Easier pedaling and faster rotations signal the time to shift up a gear or two to keep pedal strokes even and to move ahead faster. Repeat as needed to maintain cadence and speed.

front pedal sprocket rings

If a subsequent descent is followed by a climb, reposition gears by moving again to a smaller front sprocket ring and to a higher rear gear— one of the smaller outside rings.

rear wheel sprocket rings

Extended Uphills

Many novice cyclists dread extended uphills and dismount almost before they begin to climb. But there are good ways to cope with ascending trails and roads. Give these various techniques a try; you can always bail out later.

Look ahead as you ride and prepare for a long climb by adjusting gear positions as you approach the upgrade. See "Rolling Terrain" for specifics about gear relationships, functions and positions. Timing is crucial for success: Downshifting too soon leads to "pedaling air," the loss of footing on pedals, and a slowed momentum;

shifting too late or making a big change in gear ratios increases tension and can result in a chain flying off a ring.

Pace yourself. For all climbs, accelerate on the downslopes or level sections to acquire momentum. For the longest ascents, take it easy at the start, waiting until you are warmed up and your pulse is elevated before cranking up. Save some energy for the final push. And for climbs of an hour or more, raise your seat for full leg extension and more power.

On steep uphills, all cyclists should shift body weight slightly forward to keep the front wheel in contact with the riding surface. Weight should be centered between front and rear. While a little forward lean is fine, do not assume a prone position; this constricts the diaphragm and impedes deep breathing. You need more oxygen, not less. Keep elbows bent out slightly to open the chest.

On extended climbs, less athletic cyclists will find the slowest ascent to be least taxing for the legs because of minimal resistance. Sit atop the seat while spinning your pedals at a fast rate in low gear. Anticipate the hill and use your left shifter to move to the smallest sprocket ring in front, the "granny gear." Engage the highest gear in back and downshift when needed with your right shifter to keep your cadence steady.

Stronger riders may prefer to "grind" in a middle gear and pedal at a moderate rate. You will move along faster this way, but your legs will work harder against the increased resistance. For this technique, slide back on the saddle to best utilize arm and back muscles and to apply force sooner at the top of the pedal stroke. Unless you are a great athlete, it is difficult to muscle uphill for miles. Such a push can result in cramps and burnout.

Standing up to pedal uses your body weight to push down and your arms to pull up in opposition. It also relieves muscle tension in legs. Standing is a good technique for breaking up long ascents or topping off a hill when you have run through all your low gears. If you do stand on your pedals, shift first to a higher gear to have some crank resistance for power and balance. Your cadence will be slow. At first, a standing position may feel awkward and be hard to sustain, but practice brings rapid improvement.

Stop or walk your bike when you run out of gas. Enjoy the scenery. Isn't that why you are here? Just one minute of rest will make a difference. And if you tank up on a sport drink enriched with calories and electrolytes, you will get the boost you need.

Downhills

Descending from the Maroon Bells or Ashcroft is a big rush—a giddy freedom. On these and all paved roads, cyclists can build up tremendous speed. The ride is both exhilarating and dangerous. Control is critical.

The faster you travel, the farther you should be from the road's edge. Take a position in the middle of the right lane. Drop your bike seat if the descent is very steep, move far back on the saddle, and maintain a low stance. Flex knees and elbows to absorb bumps; think of them as shock absorbers. These adjustments give a feeling of security and mastery.

To moderate your speed, apply both brakes gradually, pulling first and pulling harder on the right/rear brake. (A strong pull on the left/front brake alone will catapult you over the handlebars.) To save some wear on those brakes and still slow yourself down, utilize wind resistance: Sit up straight and stick your knees out. This may not look cool, but it works.

For lean on curves, set the outside foot in the lowest pedal position and angle a knee, elbow or both toward the inside of the turn.

Always be cautious if you do not know the territory. And be watchful for changes in familiar terrain. The sudden appearance of a wild animal, a fallen rock, a new patch of gravel or a wet pavement is a very real hazard on mountain roads. A fast turn on gravel absolutely guarantees disaster.

While descents on paved roads focus on managing speed, descents over rough terrain are major workouts for muscles and help to improve coordination, balance and reflexes. If you ride the chairlifts up the area's ski mountains, you face some hairy slopes. Such downhills require modification of techniques.

Your concern on 4wd roads and singletracks will be with body and pedal positions and with choice of route. Forget sitting down. Instead, shift your weight back by pushing your hips behind the seat; this minimizes your profile, improves control and curtails saddle pain. Keep cranks parallel to the ground to avoid striking stones or scraping surfaces on curves. Time pedal rotations to clear obstructions. Maintain momentum to pass over obstacles—pedal through. Stay alert, scanning ahead for the best route over ruts, rocks and deadfall. Pray for divine guidance. Check your grip on the handlebars; if it is too tight, the rest of your body will tense up. Breathe deeply. Just try to keep physically and mentally relaxed.

BRAKING

Skillful braking is a study in subtlety. Finesse often means restraint. Overdo braking and you will create your own accident. But apply some simple techniques and you will return home unscathed.

1. Use the front/left brake with caution: It is very effective. A sharp pull could vault you over the handlebars on a downhill run. Never lock that front wheel.

2. Apply rear/right brakes first, before engaging front.

3. Pull harder on the rear brake, especially on descents. Try to make this a routine action.

4. When braking on downhills, drop your torso and move back on the saddle, thus placing more weight over the rear wheel and countering the forward momentum of stopping.

5. Plan ahead for a sharp curve and slow down before the turn. Then ease off brakes and cruise or pedal through the corner.

6. On extended downhills, vary brake pressure to avoid heating up brakes, rims and tires.

7. Practice braking in a variety of conditions so that your response will be automatic.

SAFETY & ETIQUETTE

ROAD RIDING

Many of the cycling tours in this guide follow two-lane, country byways. These routes were selected for their wonderful scenery and light motor vehicle traffic. In these surroundings, it is easy to become relaxed and chatty as you ride. But because the roads are narrow, serpentine and often without shoulders, staying alert means staying unhurt. Cycle defensively, anticipate dangerous situations, and never assume that a motorist has seen you.

Rules of the Road

Colorado law gives motorists and bicyclists equal rights and responsibilities on public roadways. A state campaign, complete with road signs, emphasizes *sharing* the road—a response, most likely, to the growing popularity of cycling in Colorado. The point is that drivers and bikers need to be considerate of each other so that road travel can be enjoyable and safe.

Motorists are required to pass cyclists with care, leaving at least three feet between their vehicles and the riders. Any harassment or reckless endangerment by a motorist is a misdemeanor offense and should be reported to the police.

Bicycle riders are likewise expected to adhere to certain rules which eliminate confusion and protect life.

1. Ride on the paved shoulders of roads, and when no shoulder exists, ride as far to the right as possible.

2. Cycle with the flow of traffic, not against it.

3. Use standard hand signals to warn motorists and other cyclists of your intentions.

      left turn   right turn   slow/stop

4. When turning left, position yourself in the roadway as you would in an automobile, and extend your left arm to signal. If this move is uncomfortable, cycle to the crosswalk and ride or walk your bike through the intersection.

5. Ride single file when an overtaking vehicle reaches a distance of 300 feet to your rear or if visibility is limited to 300 feet front or rear. This sight distance limitation is common on Colorado's winding roads.

6. You may always ride two or more abreast on the shoulder if the shoulder width is adequate.

Passing

Signs posted on many local roads display a bicycle symbol and the words "Single File." They occur in places where visibility is poor, where a shoulder is absent and/or where moderate traffic can be expected. It is smart to heed the warning. Other behaviors can also protect riders from passing motor vehicles.

1. In constricted lanes or when approaching an intersection, it may be better to ride in the middle of the lane to be more visible and to prevent sideswipes by motorists. "Taking a lane" can be safer than staying to the right in a spot where two cars cannot pass comfortably. A driver may be tempted to squeeze by you, and along a cliff edge or ditch, you have nowhere to go. Always look around carefully before taking a lane, and return to the road's right side when conditions improve.

2. When biking with a group on an especially narrow road with considerable traffic, spread out so that cars can safely weave around each rider. Put about 50 yards between cyclists.

3. When a bulky RV or large truck inches up from the rear, expect it to be followed by a long column of frustrated drivers. Pull over, let them all pass, and then relish some solitude.

4. If cars pile up behind you on a twisting mountain road where passing is unwise, stop, move aside and allow the whole queue to advance.

5. When cyclists are traveling together, the last rider in line should warn of a vehicle approaching from the rear. Call out "car back" or "car behind" and pass the word forward so everyone can move to single file. The rider on the left should accelerate to form the single string; falling back is risky because of other riders and the approaching car.

6. When passing cars that are parked parallel to the pavement's edge, put distance between you and the vehicle to avoid doors suddenly opened in your path.

7. 4wd roads are usually skinny, rutted tracks that may edge a ravine or ascend over boulders. Maneuverable mountain bikes share these precipitous routes with less agile jeeps and all-terrain vehicles. In a hazardous spot, pull over to let the larger vehicle negotiate the terrain. In any encounter with a truck or jeep in the backcountry, inform the driver of your group's size.

Trail Riding

The advantage of trail riding is immediately obvious: Free of threatening, exhaust-belching cars, trucks and RVs, cyclists can relax in a safer, cleaner, more tranquil environment. Most of the trail riding covered in this guide is over paved surfaces. But paved or dirt, trail travel has special characteristics and requires special etiquette.

While motorized vehicles are absent, horses, hikers, in-line skaters and other cyclists are not. Self-preservation on roads is replaced by attention to manners on trails. As trail users are generally more concerned with recreation than with speed, a sharing attitude is common. But bicycles can be intimidating. With awareness and considerate behavior, cyclists can reduce the anxiety of others.

1. Yield the right-of-way to pedestrians. And when approaching from behind, alert walkers, runners and in-line-skaters to your presence *in advance* and tell them on which side you intend to pass. For instance, call out, "passing on the left." Use a bell if you have one. Pedestrians frequent the Rio Grande Trail, the Golf Course Loop, all Snowmass Village trails and the path through Glenwood Canyon.

2. Yield the right-of-way to horses. They are easily spooked by bikers and hikers. Leave the trail quietly and allow the horses to pass. You and the equestrians will be much safer. If approaching from behind, slow down, alert the riders, wait until their mounts are brought under control, wait for a signal to pass, and then walk your bike past the group.

3. Yield to approaching mountain bikers if they are ascending: It is difficult to regain momentum on a climb. If approaching from behind, notify the biker as you would notify a pedestrian. Should faster cyclists want to pass you, yield by moving to the edge of the trail.

4. Slow down or stop when encountering wild or domestic animals. Give them a chance to retreat without panic.

5. Respect the private property that often borders recreational paths. Do not trespass or toss litter.
6. If you venture into the backcountry, stay on trails. Off-trail riding contributes to erosion, especially in muddy conditions; it destroys fragile mountain flora; and it frightens wildlife, which has more than enough problems with human encroachment. Stay off routes reserved for horses or hikers only. And *always* turn back at a Wilderness Area sign: All mechanized vehicles are banned by law from designated wilderness.

GROUP RIDING

A bicycle outing with friends constitutes a party. Pedaling off to an alfresco brunch or lunch is a delicious diversion. But this celebration on wheels also presents some complications. Riders can run into each other, and often do; someone can get detached from the group; and with no riding rules, confusion is possible. With the goal of getting everyone happily to the destination and back, a bit of organization is recommended.

1. The leader, or forward rider, is responsible for giving hand signals, warning of hazards, deciding where to pause for breaks, and counting noses.
2. The rear rider, or "sweep," should be an experienced cyclist with good roadside repair and coaching skills. Patience with and empathy for the novice rider are invaluable qualities.
3. When intending to pause, the leader should hold a hand high and yell "stopping." Other riders should pass the word back to avoid rear-end collisions.
4. More collisions and confusion can be averted if the leader gives clear hand signals and calls out "right turn" or "left turn."
5. At major intersections, the group should pull off the road or trail and wait for the "sweep" to catch up. Count noses and check on everyone's condition, energy and water supply.

6. All riders who notice trouble—broken glass, a pothole, low branches, an aggressive dog—should sound a noisy alert to companions.

7. The last cyclist in line must warn of a rear-approaching vehicle by calling out "car back." As the word is passed forward, riders should form a single column for safety.

❧

"What is more beautiful than a road?"

—George Sand

1 Aspen West End Tour

Holden-Marolt Mining & Ranching Museum

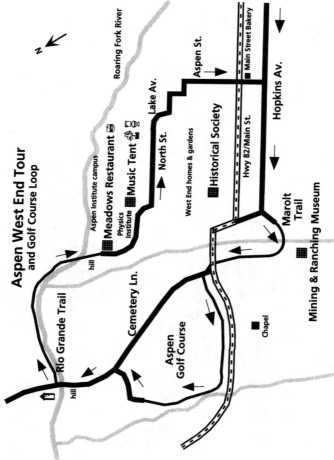

ASPEN WEST END TOUR
and Golf Course Loop

Ride Distance:	4.8 miles for basic circle tour
Route Type:	Loop with variations
Elevation Change:	191 feet
Riding Surface:	Paved streets, paved trail, dirt trail
Terrain:	Flat with one hill near river
Amenities:	Restaurants, water, restrooms, bike shops
Highlights:	Museums, Music Tent, historic homes, gardens
Tour Extension:	East of Aspen Bonus Ride

THIS EASY CIRCLE TOUR invites cyclists to travel quiet streets and bicycle trails from Aspen's center to its various West End neighborhoods. It meanders over Castle Creek to the Holden-Marolt Mining and Ranching Museum, around the Aspen Golf Course and down Cemetery Lane, over the Roaring Fork River and along the Rio Grande Trail, and past the Aspen Institute campus, the Music Tent, and 19th century Victorian homes and gardens. A leisurely, follow-your-fancy circuit is recommended for the residential streets, with a suggested pause at the Aspen Historical Society.

Amenities, such as bike rentals and alfresco cafés, cluster in Aspen's downtown. But alone in the West End, on the campus of the Aspen Institute, the Meadows Restaurant patio is all serenity: a garden bower inviting private conversation.

Access by Bicycle: Pedal to Hopkins Avenue, which is parallel to and one block south of Main Street. Ride Hopkins west into a residential area. The street is a designated bikeway with scant automobile traffic.

Access by Car: Leave your vehicle in the Rio Grande parking garage on Mill Street, one block downhill from Main. The ride's start is on Hopkins Avenue, one block south of Main and two blocks from the garage. (P)

0.0 **Turn left onto 7th Street where Hopkins ends.** Mounted here are a green bike route sign and a brown sign directing riders left for the Music School, the AABC and Snowmass.

Bear right onto the Marolt Trail at a large brown and gold sign. Arrows point toward Cemetery Lane and Castle Creek Road. A large Aspen Area Trails and Bike Routes map is mounted in a frame. The paved path drops downhill to cross Marolt Bridge over Castle Creek.

0.2 **At a trail junction west of the bridge, continue straight** toward Castle Creek Road **to visit the Mining and Ranching Museum,** immediately adjacent to the path.

> ### HOLDEN-MAROLT MINING AND RANCHING MUSEUM
>
> The museum, established by the Aspen Historical Society in 1989, consists of several aged buildings and an informal scattering of farm and mine equipment. A large placard standing before the largest structure—originally a sampling building for ore—presents some remarkable old photographs and a written history of the site: a history illustrating the story of Aspen itself. At this writing, the museum is entirely an informal, outdoor experience, but the AHS plans many enhancements.

To continue the West End Tour, turn right at the junction toward Cemetery Lane. Castle Creek dashes through a ravine to the right.

0.3 **Bear right** at another sign for Cemetery Lane, cycle under Highway 82 **and pedal up** a short rise, following the bike route sign.

0.5 **Pedal ahead to cross Cemetery Lane** at Bugsy Barnard Park, a pretty little place with a pond and picnic table. **Bear left** on the bike path to circle the Aspen Golf Course. ✇

Ride parallel to Route 82 alongside a rustic fence. Hayden Peak is glimpsed through a notch in the mountains left of the Highlands ski area. Red Butte juts above the golf course.

1.2 As you approach the golf course entrance, Pyramid Peak at left is beautifully framed by the Highlands and Buttermilk ski areas.

1.3 **Pedal straight ahead** to continue the loop. Do *not* cross the bridge. The loop path will meld into Chatfield Road, a quiet enclave where houses face the golf course.

1.8 Follow Homestake, edging the golf course. It flows into Silverking Drive.

2.2 **Turn left onto Cemetery Lane** and cruise downhill to cross Slaughterhouse Bridge over the Roaring Fork. ⌂

2.7 **Turn right onto the Rio Grande Trail**, a paved, riverside path named for the narrow-gauge railroad that once served the valley. The lively water makes this a wonderful stretch of trail.

3.3 **Bear right at a sign for Picnic Point Bridge,** 8th Street and the Meadows. The arched bridge over the river is a special place.

Both forks in the dirt trail ahead lead sharply uphill to the Aspen Institute's Meadows complex, a 40-acre site of Bauhaus-inspired buildings and stylish landscaping. Both routes are challenging and may require you to dismount. The right fork is the designated bike route, but the wider, shorter left trail is recommended here.

The big homes of Red Mountain are visible as you follow an S-curve uphill to a paved lane fronting townhomes overlooking Castle Creek. Pedal a short distance to Meadows Drive.

3.6 **The Meadows Restaurant patio** is a flower-bedecked retreat cached below and adjacent to the Bandar bin Sultan Center.

Meadows Restaurant

Behind a leafy screen at the foot of stone steps, the patio of the Meadows Restaurant resembles a secret garden. Encircled by wildflowers and blessed with an awesome mountain view, it seems an antidote for anxiety. Its clientele includes participants in the Aspen Institute's seminars. If early morning cyclists find the patio chilly, they may sample breakfast in the large adjacent dining room. A buffet of both hot and cold items is offered midday, and a Continental-American-Vietnamese menu provides distinctive choices at dinner.

Summer Hours: Breakfast, 7 to 9:30 am; lunch, noon to 2 pm; dinner, 6 to 9 pm daily.

Etc: Credit cards. Dinner reservations advised.

Telephone: 925-4240

Three attractive routes shepherd you to the Music Tent. An **artistic pedestrian path** connects this Institute cluster to Aspen Institute seminar buildings, the Paepcke Auditorium and the Tent. If you choose this graceful byway past sculpture, grassy mounds, a pond and the Elizabeth Paepcke Memorial Wildflower Garden, **please walk your bike**.

To cycle directly to the Tent, pick up a path across from the restaurant and bear left to ride high above the Roaring Fork River for 0.3 miles. **For more of a tour,** continue on the Meadows Drive/8th Street bikeway past tennis courts to

North Street. The distant alpine view is of the Independence Pass region.

3.7 **Bear left from the bikeway onto North Street and left again on 5th Street.**

4.1 **Stop at the Tent** for a musical interlude. Many rehearsals and concerts are free. Should one be underway, slip quietly inside to listen. Or lounge and picnic on the lawn for any performance. The tent area includes a snack stand, a Music Festival gift shop, and the Joan and Irving Harris Concert Hall, a superb performance facility.

> ### BAYER-BENEDICT MUSIC TENT
>
> The Music Tent is the original home of the Aspen Music Festival. Now a nine-week concert extravaganza, the festival sprang from Aspen's 1949 Goethe Bicentennial celebration. This tent, replacing the original designed by Eero Saarinen and a 1964 successor by Herbert Bayer, bears the names of two architects whose extraordinary work has given style and individuality to modern Aspen: Herbert Bayer, trained at Walter Gropius' Bauhaus School, and Fritz Benedict, a student of Frank Lloyd Wright. Both respected architects were involved in the design of the Aspen Institute's Meadows campus, unmistakably Bauhaus in its clean functionalism.

Depart the Music Tent to begin a **personal exploration** of the lovely and eclectic West End. Here, on peaceful streets, are restored miners' cottages, the Victorian mansions of Aspen's founders, rustic ski retreats of the 1950s, new luxury homes, and enchanting gardens.

Aspen Historical Society

The Aspen Historical Society lies between 5th and 6th Streets on Bleeker, one block short of Main. It occupies the Wheeler-Stallard House, a brick Queen Anne residence that Eastern investor Jerome Wheeler built in 1889, the same year that he financed the Jerome Hotel and Wheeler Opera House. But Wheeler's wife, Harriet Macy Valentine of the New York merchandising family, showed no interest in Aspen, and so others occupied the elegant home until it was purchased by Mary Stallard in 1917. Walter Paepcke, father of Aspen's Renaissance, acquired the structure in 1945. The Aspen Historical Society, owner since 1969, has filled the rooms and grounds with fragments of Aspen's past. Its archives, preservation work and historical tours benefit valley residents and visitors. Open afternoons, T-Fri. 925-3721.

For **a direct return to midtown,** depart the tent's grounds on the east side. Turn left on Gillespie Street which bends right to become Lake Avenue. This route is reserved for bicycles and pedestrians only. Markers guide you past charming homes, Triangle Park, the Given Biomedical Institute and the Arts & Recreation Center. Several left turns will carry you to Aspen Street.

4.8 **Cross Main Street on Aspen** at the traffic signal to revisit Hopkins Avenue and the loop's start.

Drink Tip

Charlie Tarver, owner of The Hub bike shop, warns that containers of bottled water are not sized for the cages installed on mountain bikes. They frequently fall out unnoticed, littering the landscape and leaving cyclists dry. Investing a few dollars in a standard bike bottle is good for the environment and good for you.

Aspen Alfresco

You are in Aspen, and your thoughts have turned to food and drink. Inviting eateries seem to be everywhere, making the cuisine scene a bit overwhelming. But by setting parameters, the decision process becomes somewhat manageable. What follows is a modest tally of restaurants, bakery cafés and coffeeshops which offer outdoor seating for breakfast, lunch or snacks and which fall into Aspen's low to moderate price range. Select for ambiance or menu and then fuel up for a downvalley jaunt or reward yourself after a ride from Snowmass Village.

Bagel Bites
300 Puppy Smith St.

This busy, shortstop café is the flagship operation for a locally owned small chain. An extended family operates several outlets in the valley and supplies bagels to about 30 restaurants, hotels and grocery stores. The bakery's ovens are in Basalt, and they turn out an awesome variety of bagel delights, including bagel chips to accompany sandwiches. The family has also developed original cream cheese recipes such as spinach artichoke, maple macadamia, fresh strawberry, and cilantro green chile. If bagels are not your thing, stop by for Bud's Mud, the café's homemade ice cream. And if you have trouble making decisions, the list of fruit smoothie options might be an overload. Munch at an outdoor table or pack a bike bag with hefty bagel sandwiches or bagel "power bars," always good travelers.

Diner Favorites: Bagel with Garden Veggie cream cheese, Egg with Cheese Breakfast Bagel, Oven Roasted Turkey Sandwich, fruit smoothies, "Power Bar" bagel.

Summer Hours: 7:30 am to 8 pm weekdays; 8 am to 6 pm weekends.

Etc: Cash and local checks only. Takeout.

Telephone: 920-3489

Boogie's Diner
534 E. Cooper at Hunter St.

Boogie's celebrates 1950s America. And savvy locals know that indulging in Boogie's milkshakes is the most delicious way to revel in the past. Noteworthy for its mashed potatoes, Boogie's also offers up The Monster Mash Meat Loaf Dinner, Ahi and Harriet Sandwich, Chubby Checker Chicken Fingers appetizers, Elvis' Hound Dog and hot drinks with names like The Tab Hunter and The Hula Hoop. Music of the decade is piped onto the spacious balcony where the usual street scene is replaced by tops of trees, mountains and downtown buildings. Green umbrellas shade white tables, and flowers fill boxes lining the outside wall. But Boogie's is not entirely retro. It sets a foot in the present by loading its menu with lean meats, dolphin-safe tuna and items labeled as heart-healthy. To reach the restaurant, mount a staircase from Boogie's trendy clothing boutique at street level.

Diner Favorites: At lunch, all burgers, summer salads, Hot Open-faced Turkey Sandwich with mashed potatoes, gravy, cole slaw and cranberry sauce.

Summer Hours: 11 am to 10 pm daily.

Etc: Child's portions. Credit cards. Full bar.

Telephone: 925-6610

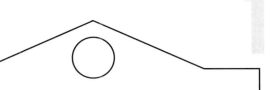

Café Ink!
520 E. Durant Ave. on the lower level, inside D&E

A coffee bar inside a snowboard shop? That's right. This little oasis may not be especially visible, but it serves up the best mocha freeze around and complements it with fresh bagels, banana bread, peach tarts, panini, sandwiches and more. Iced chai, smoothies and fat-free shakes are also on the menu. Inside are couches, small tables and an assortment of teas, beans, and mugs for sale. Add a pleasant below-street patio, and it's worth the stop. Café Ink! is also found on the Snowmass Village Mall.

Diner Favorites: Ice-blended Black (mocha) or White (latte); espresso shakes made with yogurt and milk; protein yogurt smoothies made with fruit and orange juice.

Summer Hours: 6:30 am to 11 pm every day of year.

Etc: Cash, local checks, Traveler's Checks.

Telephone: 544-0588

Cantina
411 E. Main at Mill St.

This busy Mexican restaurant could be called Aspen's hub, both geographically and socially. Smack in the middle of town, it is terrific for people-watching and is a magnet for visitors anytime and locals faithful to the daily Happy Hour. To reach the brick patio, pass through Cantina's generous interior—a subtle evocation of Old Mexico with square floor tiles, wood beams, brick walls, baskets and pottery. The large outdoor alcove is partitioned from Main Street's sidewalk by a metal fence and planter; a trellis-like roof wears tiny colored lights, hanging pots overflow with trailing blossoms, and a massing of greenery in the patio's center suggests a fountain or a pyramid. Indoors, Cantina tees and baseball caps are for sale to devoted patrons.

Diner Favorites: At lunch, Puebla Grilled Chicken Salad, Chimichanga, all quesadillas, the daily specials.

Summer Hours: 11 am to 10:30 pm daily.

Etc: Child's menu. Credit cards. No reservations. Happy Hour, 3 to 7 pm.

Telephone: 925-3663

Explore Booksellers & Bistro
221 E. Main St.

Explore is unlike any other Aspen dining establishment. This bookstore in an old Victorian residence is also the town's only completely vegetarian restaurant. It serves up sophisticated, international cuisine made with a vast array of organic ingredients. Even the water is filtered and deionized. But Explore's ambiance is special too. Indoors, classical music sets the tone; antique tables and chairs are tucked into book-lined alcoves and anterooms; flowered, fringed shawls drape over lace window curtains; a richly pattered carpet, red napkins and green wallpaper enhance the Victorian look. Outdoors, the second-floor deck seems an airy tree house, a secret hideout in the middle of Aspen. Round garden tables, blooming geraniums and a pervasive calm combine for a lovely extension to the elegant interior. Brunch is served until closing, desserts are to die for, black bean soup occupies a permanent place on the menu, and drinks both hot and cold are too numerous to count.

Diner Favorites: At lunch, Garden Burgers, omelettes, Lentil Pâté Appetizer, daily specials.

Summer Hours: "Late am to late pm" daily.

Etc: Child's menu. Credit cards. Beer & wine.

Telephone: 925-5338

Flying Dog Brew Pub
424 E. Cooper at Galena on the Mall

This place is fun. With a choice of two different outdoor venues and a delightfully doggy interior, everyone finds a comfortable spot to let down and eat (and drink) up. The best rubbernecking is from a sidewalk table on the Cooper Avenue mall. A sunken courtyard far below the street holds trees, a fountain and more tables. Beyond the courtyard lies the brew pub's interior and a quirky decor devoted to dogs. Exhibited is a vast collection of dog photos, cartoons, posters and wood carvings. Tee shirts feature canines or other small breweries. There is a dog tapestry and a dog piñata. And behind a huge glass window are mash barrels, sacks of malt, and equipment used in the first stage of the brewing process. If a post-ride brew seems right, sample Ol' Yeller Golden Ale, the gold medal Doggie Style Amber Ale, porters, stouts or seasonal beers. The broad lunch menu (illustrated with English dog engravings, what else?) includes Limousin beef, 87% lean and low in cholesterol.

Diner Favorites: At lunch, French Dip Sandwich, Limousin Burger, salads, the daily lunch special served with beer or soda, fries, salad and mashed potatoes.

Summer Hours: 11:30 am to 10 pm daily (for food).

Etc: Child's menu. Credit cards. No checks. Full menu takeout. Full bar.

Telephone: 925-7464

Main Street Bakery Café
201 E. Main at Aspen St.

Just down the block from Explore is another Old West relic. Flat-roofed, square and squat, the masonry structure dates from the late 1880s. The bakery building out back was once a brothel with six tiny rooms, each equipped with a narrow bed, a stove and a door to the outside. Today the Main Street Bakery Café welcomes families and hums with activity. Patrons give in to temptation at the bakery case or sample American home cooking for breakfast, lunch or dinner. Mornings are very big at the café, with the takeout line often extending to the sidewalk. Most business comes from people looking for something from the pastry case: turnovers, scones, elephant ears, Chocolate Chambord Cake, Apple Bourbon Bread Pudding, Linzer Torte.... Inside, lemon water sits on small wood tables, a blackboard lists coffees and teas, and two huge wall units from an old Missouri pharmacy hold local jellies and sauces, Krabloonik soups and clay muffin pots. Outside, green umbrellas hover over an assortment of tables set on a concrete patio and on the grass. Trees and shrubs surround the spacious yard; yarrow, cosmos, petunias and mint grow in borders and in planters.

Diner Favorites: House coffees, lattes, donuts, herbal iced tea, soups, Open-faced Veggie Sandwich with hummus, guacamole, or basil-goat cheese.

Summer Hours: 7 am to 9:30 pm daily.

Etc: Child's menu at dinner. Credit cards. Beer & wine.

Telephone: 925-6446

Mezzaluna
624 E. Cooper Ave.

Local wisdom says that Mezzaluna is a people-watching mecca: a chic, sophisticated spot to play both reviewer and performer. The sunny patio fronting Cooper's sidewalk is certainly public. But it is lovely too: A modern, sculptural fountain contributes pleasant water sounds; flowers encircle trees in brick and tile planters; contemporary yellow chairs and square green tables sit under natural canvas umbrellas. Inside, tall yuccas stand by tall windows which open like doors to the street and patio. Breezy and cool, it seems an extension of outdoors. The blue ceiling is painted with pink clouds; pink marble tables match the pink

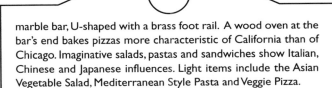

marble bar, U-shaped with a brass foot rail. A wood oven at the bar's end bakes pizzas more characteristic of California than of Chicago. Imaginative salads, pastas and sandwiches show Italian, Chinese and Japanese influences. Light items include the Asian Vegetable Salad, Mediterranean Style Pasta and Veggie Pizza.

Diner Favorites: At lunch, Half Moon Caesar Salad, Spaghettini with Roma Tomatoes, Penne Pasta with Rock Shrimp, Grilled Chicken Breast with Jicama, Blackened Ahi Tuna Salad.

Summer Hours: 11:30 am to 11 pm daily.

Etc: Child's portions. Credit cards. Happy Hour and $5 pizzas, 3 to 5:30 pm.

Telephone: 925-5882

Paradise Bakery & Café
320 S. Galena at Cooper

Abuzz all summer, this pocket-size, high-traffic snackery offers up giant fresh-baked muffins, cookies, croissants and brownies; espresso, latte, cappuccino and fresh-squeezed lemonade; homemade Italian-style ice cream, gelati and frozen yogurt—nonfat and otherwise. At breakfast there are bagel sandwiches and specialty cream cheeses. Thick, 12-inch, chocolate chip cookies can be made and decorated to order in two hours. Indoor counter space is tiny; patrons, often with their bikes, dogs or children, congregate on benches on the sidewalk plaza to enjoy good fare and the colorful street scene. Huge planters overflow with flowers and vines. If a bike ride has sapped your energy, a quick stop at Paradise will handle the problem.

Diner Favorites: Chocolate chip cookies, low-fat raspberry muffins, fresh-squeezed lemonade.

Summer Hours: 6:30 am to midnight daily.

Etc: Cash and checks only.

Telephone: 925-7585

The Popcorn Wagon
301 S. Mill at Hyman on the Mall

This eatery is entirely alfresco. Park your bike and order crêpes, sandwiches, hot dogs, soups, chili and popcorn from the wagon's windows. Look for this red and yellow mini-café near the spurting fountain and across from the Opera House. White metal café tables shaded by umbrellas are tucked behind aspens growing from brick planters. Crêpes are the specialty here: meaty choices, all-veggie, and chocolate, cinnamon or fruit varieties flamed in brandy. This is a no-stress environment for children and their parents. And the neighboring fountain, designed for water-play, is irresistible.

Diner Favorites: Turkey Crêpes, Vegetarian Crêpes, Greegaros, hot popcorn.

Summer Hours: 11 am to 2 am daily.

Etc: Cash only.

Telephone: 925-2718

Pour la France!
413 E. Main at Mill St.

Rated one of the top breakfast spots in America, this French bistro and café bustles all day. Next door to the Cantina in the center of Aspen, its alluring patio beckons passersby. Blue awnings and blue and white tablecloths and umbrellas amplify the French theme. Flowers separate the alfresco dining space from the sidewalk. Inside are brick walls, French posters, fresh blossoms on tables and a prominent pastry case. Enticing fruit tarts, scones, pies and cheesecakes may motivate you to bike a few extra miles. Most popular are the tarts and "anything chocolate." Cappuccino comes in capacious cups brimming with "the best foam in Aspen." Healthy items include panini—a low-fat sandwich prepared in a European press. Pour la France will pack picnic fare for all-day adventures.

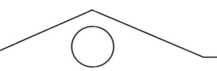

Diner Favorites: At breakfast, Eggs Aspen, Eggs Benedict, omelette du jour. At lunch, Panini served with Caesar Salad, Poached Salmon Niçoise and Vegetarian Niçoise Salads, soup/salad/sandwich combos.

Summer Hours: 7 am to 9 pm daily in "high season."

Etc: Child's menu. Credit cards. Full bar.

Telephone: 920-1151

The Red Onion
420 E. Cooper on the Mall

The Red Onion is Aspen's oldest saloon. Built as an upscale men's club by Tom Latta in during the silver boom, it has been operating in the same location since 1892. Constructed of lasting brick and embellished with some fancy ornamentation, it was a step above Western commercial structures. A carved pediment tops its tall, narrow face. The club included smoking and gaming rooms and, perhaps, a brothel upstairs. Inside, old photographs and rare tintypes chronicle the history of the Onion and of Aspen. The front room is almost unchanged since "sporting men" drank fine whiskies at its bar. Outside, a metal railing marks the perimeter of the small alfresco dining space. Like its Cooper Avenue neighbor, the Flying Dog, its mall location is perfect for checking out passersby. The food focus is on Mexican fare and American burgers, sandwiches, salads and soups. Daily lunch specials should never leave you hungry.

Diner Favorites: At lunch, all burgers, Fajitas, B.A.T. (bacon, avocado and turkey sandwich).

Summer Hours: 11 am to 10 pm daily (for food).

Etc: Child's fare. Credit cards. Happy Hour, 3:30 to 6 pm.

Telephone: 925-9043

Rusty's Hickory House Restaurant
730 W. Main St.

The antithesis of Mezzaluna's nouvelle cuisine is the fodder from the Hickory House: slabs of ribs, barbecued chicken, baked beans, mashed potatoes, gravy. The owner, a native Kentuckian, has a simple philosophy: "My mamma told me never let a customer leave hungry." This is not pre-exercise food, but it may satisfy certain hearty appetites after a long day of biking. The owner's team has won 29 international rib cooking competitions over a seven-year period. In 1996 it made history by capturing the two big titles at the planet's largest ribfest: "Best Ribs in the World" and "Best Barbecue Sauce in the World." Breakfast and lunch have long been popular with locals, but light food is lightly represented. In a log building at the west end of Main St., the restaurant serves outdoors on the porch and patio. Unpeeled log railings give the place a rustic, early Aspen look.

Diner Favorites: At breakfast, Breakfast Burritos, Fruit Pancakes, Huevos Rancheros. At lunch, hickory-smoked pork and beef sandwiches, ribs.

Summer Hours: 6 am to 2:30 pm daily; dinner at 5 pm.

Etc: Credit cards. Full bar.

Telephone: 925-2313

Wienerstube Restaurant
633 E. Hyman near Spring St.

One visit to the "Stube" and you will understand why it has been an Aspen favorite since 1965. Stop for an Austrian or American breakfast or lunch, or pamper yourself anytime with the Viennese pastries. Outside, flowerboxes dripping with petunias, geraniums and pansies embrace the deck and adorn the front entrance. An awning and aspens shade alfresco diners. Inside are skylights and ficus trees, international flags and stained glass.

And more flowers—alive, in photographs, in paintings, on the wallpaper. Austrian furnishings and lace café curtains add to the charm. A large locals' table contributes to a family feeling. The pastry case is a big distraction. It is laden with delicacies such as Austrian Cherry Gateaux and Chafoutis, Wiener Nusstorte, Konigscknitte and Sacher Torte. Most popular is the Black Forest Torte, and most endearing are the Truffle Mice. All are made on site. Light, healthy items appear on both breakfast and lunch menus. Each day, special salads and fish are announced, and in summer, both a cold and hot soup are featured.

Diner Favorites: At breakfast, Eggs Benedict, Corned Beef Hash, and a daily special such as German Apple Pancake or Palatschinken, a European crêpe filled with blueberries and cream cheese. At lunch, Veal Bratwurst, Wienerschnitzel, Gravad Lax.

Summer Hours: 7 am to 2:30 pm; closed Mondays.

Etc: Child's portions. Credit cards. Full bar.

Telephone: 925-3357

Zélé Gourmet Coffee
121 S. Galena at Hopkins Ave.

Zélé bills itself as "Aspen's Original European Espresso and Juice Bar." This busy spot is that—and more. The liquid fare may dominate, but Zélé makes certain that it need not be enjoyed alone. The "Daily Rush" lists coffees of the day. Enhance with an Italian syrup, or go for organic fruit juices, smoothies or rice milk. Customers may add organic Mountain Bars or brownies; they may opt for fruit tarts, scones or muffins; or they may simply abandon themselves to the decadence of Chocolate Espresso Mousse Cake, Napoleons or eclairs. Ask about sandwiches and soups. The coffee boutique sells beans, mugs, machines and bright Zélé tee shirts. The café's interior holds a bar along the windows and tiny high tables paired with black metal chairs. Patrons settle down with newspapers and drinks at the high-profile patio tables out front.

Diner Favorites: Granitas, iced lattes, cappuccinos, iced sport tea, fresh-squeezed juices—especially "Miracle Energy," a blend of carrot, apple, celery and ginger.

Summer Hours: 7 am to 10 pm.

Etc: Credit cards.

Telephone: 925-5745

"There is no love sincerer than the love of food."

—George Bernard Shaw

BONUS

Smuggler Mountain Grind

Join the many Aspen locals dedicated to a daily fitness walk, run or bike up Smuggler Mountain. The big hill is also a magnet for 4wd vehicles and dog-walkers. Its road switchbacks over gravel, rocks and ruts. This can be an up-and-down exercise or the beginning of a loop that drops into Hunter Valley and returns to town by Red Mountain Road. The loop is *not* a jaunt for novice riders.

Access from downtown Aspen is easy. Follow Hopkins Avenue east to cross a bridge over the Roaring Fork. Make an immediate left onto Park Avenue and then bear right onto Park Circle after two blocks. At Smuggler Mountain Road there is a map of Aspen's trails and bike routes. The Smuggler Mine is visible and active. About 1.5 miles up the road is a platform for scenery appreciation. This aerial look at Aspen and its mountains is a big lure. Most bikers add more uphill by entering the woods to reach to the high point near some old mines on the Hunter Valley route; the extension gains 200 feet of elevation in a half-mile for a total of 1092 feet. Turn around or choose the loop.

This is a good morning workout as summer afternoons on the road can be hot and dusty. Evening sunsets, however, are great from the platform.

Smuggler Mountain once held two of the richest silver mines in the world: the Smuggler and the Mollie Gibson. Before silver was devalued in 1893, all such mines were active around the clock, polluting their surroundings and earning great fortunes for their owners. A year after the disastrous silver crash, a gigantic nugget, the largest ever unearthed, was pulled from the Smuggler Mine. In the last century, work has been sporadic. Silver remains in the mountain, but most of the tunnels are flooded. For a closer look, ask about guided tours of Aspen's mines.

BONUS

East of Aspen

Scheduled for completion in 1997 is a new pedestrian-bike trail which wends four miles east from Aspen to Difficult Campground. Beginning at Glory Hole Park and Ute Avenue, the path leaves town, runs parallel to Highway 82, and passes the Northstar Nature Preserve. The Aspen Parks Department is working on a plan to link the Rio Grande Trail's eastern terminus at Herron Park to Ute Avenue, creating both a sinuous riverside path through Aspen and an 11-mile, car-free route from Difficult Campground to Woody Creek.

When snow blankets Independence Pass, closing Highway 82 east of Aspen, the weather at lower elevations can be sunny and mild, perfect for a bike excursion. So locals, confident of encountering no travel-through traffic, pedal up the pass road to the snow blockade. Hard-core cyclists do share the narrow space with the cars in summer, but Independence Pass Road is a *big* uphill: Distance from Aspen to the pass itself is 20 miles with 4200 feet of elevation gain.

2 Aspen to Ashcroft

Castle Creek Valley

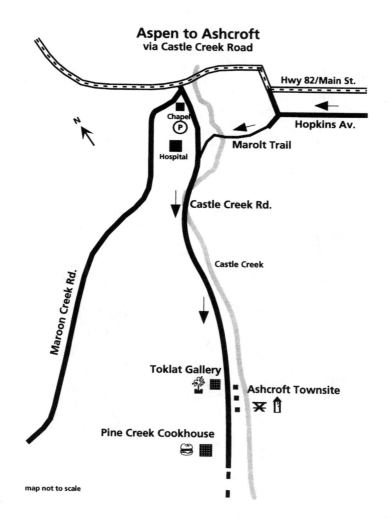

2 ASPEN TO ASHCROFT
via Castle Creek Road

Ride Distance:	23.2 miles round trip from Aspen to townsite; 21.2 from hospital
Route Type:	Out-and-back
Elevation Change:	1500 feet to townsite
Riding Surface:	Paved road and paved trail
Terrain:	Gradual grade with some dips and rises
Amenities:	Restaurant, picnic tables, water, privy
Highlights:	Stunning scenery, Ashcroft ghost town, Toklat Gallery
Tour Extensions:	Four rough 4wd roads for strong mountain bikers

THE SIMPLICITY OF THIS ROUTE allows riders to concentrate on a landscape of astonishing beauty. Castle Creek Road twists though a cool, high valley, lush with aspens and evergreens, populated by beavers and mule deer, free yet from rampant development. This extended, gradual climb to Ashcroft has many small undulations, making it an ideal ride for practicing with gears. Try gearing up and pedaling on downslopes to gain momentum for hills ahead. Ride single file: The road has countless curves and no shoulders. Turnouts invite cyclists to pull off for rest, rehydration or scenery appreciation. Beaver dams, ponds and lodges are scattered the length of the creek. And if you tire, fantasize about the long, sweet, downhill return ride.

The valley's only restaurant is the notable Pine Creek Cookhouse, a gourmet hideaway discovered years ago. Before pumping uphill to feast on food and atmosphere, call for reservations.

Departing the valley floor are Midnight Mine, Little Annie, Express Creek and Pearl Pass Roads. Steep, rutted and stone-studded, they lure mountain bikers for tests of strength, endurance and technique.

Access by Bicycle: In Aspen, pedal west on Hopkins Avenue to 7th Street. Turn left and look for the Marolt Trail on the right. Follow it across the Marolt Bridge to a sign directing you left to Castle Creek Road. You will cycle past the Holden-Marolt Mining and Ranching Museum and through the Marolt housing complex for a trip of about a mile from midtown Aspen.

Access by Car: When approaching Aspen from the west on Highway 82, turn right onto Maroon Creek Road at a traffic signal and the Aspen Chapel. Bear left immediately onto Castle Creek Road. Make the first right turn at Meadowood Drive and park in the chapel lot. Mount your bike, backtrack on Meadowood Drive and bear right immediately onto the bike path which parallels Castle Creek Road. (P)

0.0 **Begin on Castle Creek Road near Aspen Valley Hospital.** As your upvalley jaunt begins, the creek dashes through a ravine left of the route. Elevation here is 8000 feet.

0.6 Music School Road connects to a creekside campus where music students practice and perform for nine summer weeks.

1.2 Ahead is a beautiful view of Hayden Peak.

2.3 Midnight Mine Road is the first of four 4wd routes popular with experienced mountain bikers. It ascends to Aspen Mountain's summit.

4.4 Conundrum Creek Road marks the start of a long, steady uphill that may require you to shift to lower gears.

6.4 Little Annie Road climbs the backside of Aspen Mountain, connecting to Midnight Mine Road about halfway to the summit. The ascent is less precipitous than the Midnight Mine route.

9.4 The turnoff at right, opposite the handsome Elk Mountain Lodge, is a hiking route to American Lake. Devaney Creek is channeled below the road to feed Castle Creek. The valley is wide here, a marshy, flat space managed by beavers. Look for their conspicuous lodges, ponds and dams.

10.3 Express Creek Road at left is a 4wd route to Taylor Pass. Ahead are the buildings of Ashcroft ghost town.

10.6 **Ashcroft townsite and the Toklat Gallery** face each other across the road. Here, in a truly spectacular setting, are wonderful diversions. Tour the ghost town, visit the gallery in the Stuart Mace family home, or walk the Castle Creek Trail, found opposite the old Hotel View on Ashcroft's main street. Two picnic tables hide in trees at creekside. The gallery shares its pure spring water with cyclists. Elevation is 9500 feet.

> ## GHOST TOWN OF ASHCROFT
>
> Ashcroft's heyday was brief. Born in 1879 as Castle Forks silver camp, it was renamed Chloride in 1880 and vigorously hyped as a mining mecca. By 1882 the silver rush was on, and the camp was renamed again, this time for Thomas E. Ashcraft, an early booster. The next two years were big ones for the little town, but when Aspen was at its prime in 1892, Ashcroft numbered only a few hundred residents. Aspen's rich strikes, the railroads to haul its ore, flourishing social institutions and a milder climate were powerful magnets. A historical placard and a resident "ghost" can furnish intriguing details about ephemeral Ashcroft.

If you crave more than a picnic lunch, continue to the Pine Creek Cookhouse, a ride of 1.4 miles with 300 feet of elevation gain. The valley widens into wildflower meadows as you cycle toward the massive wall of snowcapped mountains that separate Ashcroft from Crested Butte.

11.6 The brown trailhead sign at right is for Cathedral Lake Trail, a wilderness hiking route.

12.0 **The Pine Creek Cookhouse** sits back from the road, overlooking an unspoiled scene.

Pine Creek Cookhouse

Summer invites midday dining on a covered deck where a musical creek and an alpine landscape enhance the culinary experience. This romantic alfresco setting, though miles from town, draws a devoted clientele. But the restaurant's warm, woodsy interior and its imaginative menu are enough to lure hedonistic diners. Ambiance and healthy, creative cuisine are a potent combination. Hungarian influence is evident in the Cold Cherry Soup and the complimentary Krozott cheese spread. Salads include ingredients such as field greens, grilled quail, salmon, portobello mushrooms and quinoa. Krisi's Brownies are pure indulgence.

Diner Favorites: Hiker's Banquet, Spinach Crêpes, Fresh Rainbow Trout, Cookhouse Decker

Summer Hours: Lunch seatings at noon and 1:30 pm; dinner at 6 and 8 pm; Sunday brunch at 11 am, 12:30 and 2 pm. Closed M and T in June and Sept.

Etc: Child's menu. Credit cards. Reservations necessary.

Telephone: 925-1044

One-half mile beyond the Cookhouse is Road 102 to Pearl Pass, a boulder-strewn artery relished by stalwart mountain bikers bound for Crested Butte. The flatter, early portion serves cross-country skiers in winter and makes a good extension for bikers who want to try riding a 4wd road.

The return trip to Aspen is exhilarating. A fast, effortless sweep, it can tempt any rider to abandon caution. But stay alert if traveling full tilt: Cars and other cyclists share the road, and deer and falling rocks can materialize suddenly. Remember to squeeze harder on the right/rear brake if you need to stop quickly: A flip over handlebars can surely spoil your day.

THE CLUNKER CONTESTS

Hanging out in Aspen leads inevitably to acquisition of a competitive spirit. This is hardly a new phenomenon. A bicycle craze in the late 1880s led to races between Aspen and Basalt. One hundred years later, when technology had produced the motorized dirt bike, a bunch of Aspenites buzzed over Pearl Pass to Crested Butte where they flaunted their achievement at the Grubstake Bar. Guys from the Grubstake countered, grabbing their old one-speed Schwinns and *pedaling* those clunkers over the pass to the Hotel Jerome Bar. A tradition was born. Even Californians journeyed to the Elk Mountains to meet the challenge. The events were festive and fun, attracting up to 100 riders. Participants dressed in bizarre outfits, camped out on the pass and chugged a lot of beer. As funkiness faded and bicycle engineering advanced, the colorful races ended. But for those mountain biking pioneers, nostalgia lingers.

*"It is not the quantity
of the meat,
but the cheerfulness
of the guests,
which makes the feast."*

—Lord Clarendon

Aspen to Maroon Bells

Maroon Bells

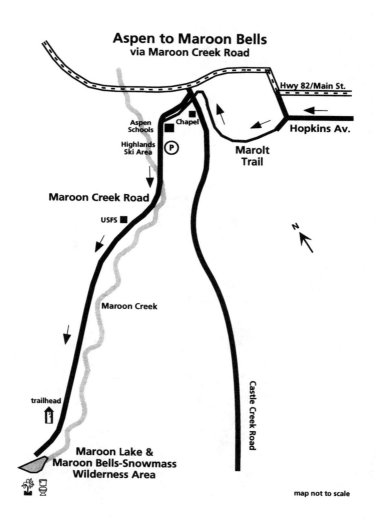

3 ASPEN TO MAROON BELLS
via Maroon Creek Road

Ride Distance:	21.2 miles round trip from Aspen; 15.4 from Highlands
Route Type:	Out-and-back
Elevation Change:	1642 feet from Aspen; 1500 from Highlands
Riding Surface:	Paved road
Terrain:	Gradual grade steepens in final 2 miles
Amenities:	Water, restrooms, bus service, shelter
Highlights:	Premier mountain landscape, guided nature tours
Tour Extension:	None. Wilderness area. No mechanized vehicles

LIKE THE ASHCROFT RIDE, the Maroon Bells tour journeys to a natural scene of intense beauty. Celebrated and recognized worldwide, the wilderness landscape at the end of Maroon Creek Road is one of the best in the West. But rewards begin as you mount your bike, for the entire route is rich with visual treasures: tantalizing looks at Pyramid Peak, wildflower meadows, fiery cliffs, avalanche chutes, comic marmots, shy mule deer. The paved road that wends upvalley is nicely graded, and while it has no shoulder, numerous turnouts and restricted daytime traffic provide security for cyclists, runners and in-line skaters.

Any effort expended in the ascent to the Bells will be forgotten in the ecstasy of the downhill run. For a one-way experience, hang your bike on an RFTA tour bus in Aspen and disembark at the ride's high point.

A picnic is an excuse to linger in this lovely place. Aspen's many delicatessens can supply simple or exotic provisions. Treat this wilderness portal with care, leaving no sign of your visit.

Access by Bicycle: In Aspen, pedal west on Hopkins Avenue to 7th Street. Turn left and look for the Marolt Trail on the right. Follow it across the Marolt Bridge to a sign directing you right, toward Cemetery Lane. Just before the path dips under Highway 82, bear left at a Maroon Creek sign to parallel the highway. The bike path crosses Castle Creek Road and carries riders past Aspen Chapel and alongside Maroon Creek Road to the campus of Aspen's public schools. Begin road riding at the large sign for the schools, approximately 1.8 miles from Mill and Main. **Cycling from midtown Aspen adds 5.8 miles to the round trip tour.**

Access by Car: From Mill and Main in central Aspen, drive west on Highway 82 for 1.3 miles. At the traffic signal and chapel, turn left onto Maroon Creek Road and continue straight ahead for 1.4 miles to the parking lot at Aspen Highlands ski area.

0.0 **Start at Aspen Highlands Ski Area** with a short downhill ride. Elevation here is 8050 feet.

0.4 Cross a bridge over Maroon Creek, which stays left of the road for the remainder of the ride.

1.1 Begin a descent to the T-Lazy-7 Ranch, formerly the Sievers homestead, a large spread dating to the 19th century.

1.6 The T-Lazy-7 is today a complex of cabins and stables. Llamas, donkeys, horses and reindeer are conspicuous in a roadside corral ahead.

1.9 A rumble strip of speed control ridges is opposite the stable. Be careful. The steady ascent to the Bells begins here.

2.3 The first of three cattle guards cuts the road. Ahead, Pyramid Peak appears and vanishes as the road bends. Aspens thrive near the sunny roadside while conifers dress the cool slopes at left.

3.4 **A National Forest entrance station** is opposite the Silver Bar Campground. Rangers turn back private automobiles between 8:30 am and 5 pm. However, tour buses may ferry visitors to the Bells from points in Aspen.

3.6 Silver Bell Campground precedes Silver Queen Campground by 1.1 miles.

4.9 East Maroon Trailhead at left is a wilderness trail for hikers and equestrians only.

5.6 The uphill grade increases from here to the ride's end. If you have not yet shifted into low gears, you will soon be tempted to do so.

6.2 At a second cattle guard and a marmot-crossing sign you have your first look at the magnificent Maroon Bells mountains. This is a perfect place to pause.

7.3 The third cattle guard bisects the pavement.

7.4 West Maroon Trailhead at right begins a wilderness tour for hikers and equestrians only.

7.7 **Maroon Lake** amenities, shelter and bus turnaround are positioned at the road's end. Elevation is 9540 feet.

The wilderness panorama before you includes a wildflower meadow, Maroon Lake and three lofty mountains rising to over 14,000 feet. These "fourteeners," craggy and built of sedimentary bands, are Pyramid Peak to the left and the two Maroon Bells at right. Avalanches and the unstable, breakaway rock of these picturesque peaks contribute to climbing deaths each year. A safer diversion is the nature trail beyond lake. Explore on your own or join a free guided walk beginning near the bus stop.

The descent to Aspen is pure bliss. But in embracing speed, know how to use your brakes and stay alert for other riders, wildlife and tour buses, especially at midday in midsummer.

While private automobiles may not approach the Bells between 8:30 am and 5 pm, vehicles may depart the Bells at any hour.

Aspen Picnic Provisions

Charcuterie & Cheese Market
665 E. Cooper, 925-8010

Gourmet everything, specialty sandwiches, custom picnic baskets.

Clark's Market
300 Puppy Smith, 925-8046

Deli, salad bar, fresh produce, sport bars, cold drinks.

Johnny McGuire's Deli
730 E. Cooper, 920-9255

Hot grilled specialty subs, sandwiches, soups, salads.

Jour de Fête
710 E. Durant, 925-3080

Sandwiches, hot lunch specials, pastries, fresh breads, juices.

Gourmet-To-Go Bistro/Café/Deli
next to Clark's, 920-3456

Sandwiches, salads, pasta, pizza, pastries, breads.

4 Snowmass Village to Aspen

Snowmass Village

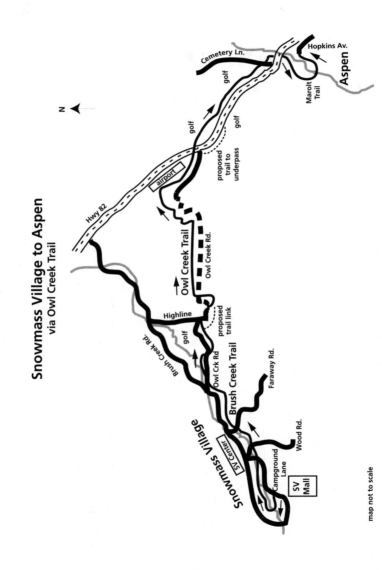

4 SNOWMASS VILLAGE TO ASPEN
via Owl Creek Trail

Ride Distance:	19.8 miles round trip from SV Mall to central Aspen
Route Type:	Out-and-back or one-way
Elevation Change:	693 feet
Riding Surface:	Paved street, paved trail, dirt road
Terrain:	Downhill most of route from SV
Amenities:	Cafés, water, restrooms, bus service, bike shops
Highlights:	Great alfresco dining, many diversions
Tour Extension:	"Snowmass Lifts" Bonus Ride

Both Snowmass Village and Aspen are rich with open-air cafés, beautiful vistas and a plethora of shops and events. Owl Creek Valley, which yokes the towns, is a spacious place of sunshine, meadows and estates. For cyclists seeking a mostly downhill, unidirectional ride, the obvious start to this tour is Snowmass Village: The Mall, at 8600 feet, is almost 700 feet higher in elevation than downtown Aspen. Popular one-way bike rentals offered by Aspen Velo, Aspen Sports and Christy Sports allow for drop-offs in either community. RFTA bus service can take you to the trailhead or return you to your start.

If you choose to begin in Aspen, just reverse the directions given below. And if you are weary when you reach the golf course, refresh at Sage, the Snowmass Club's restaurant, or put yourself and your machine on a free shuttle and be a passenger for the 600-foot climb to the Mall.

This entire tour travels paved bicycle trails with the exception of quiet Hopkins Street in Aspen and 0.8 miles of Owl Creek Road, which includes one steep, short, gravel section over Sinclair Divide. Dismount if you are uncomfortable with hills and rough surfaces. Snowmass Village planners are actively looking at ways to connect the segments of the Owl Creek Trail, thereby creating a seamless path to Aspen.

Access by Bike: Begin the trip in either Snowmass Village or Aspen.

Access by Car: In Snowmass Village, use the Mall parking lots, Base Lot A on Snowmelt Road, the lower lot at Village Center, or the Two Creeks lot on Owl Creek Road. In Aspen, stow your vehicle in the Rio Grande parking garage just off Mill Street and one block from the trailhead. (P)

- **0.0** **Start at Campground Lane and Snowmelt Road**, just below the Mall. Cycle to the far end of the adjacent parking lot to **access the Brush Creek Trail.** The woodsy, winding path traverses a bridge and parallels the creek.

- **0.7** Cross Snowmelt Road near a busy intersection, angling slightly right to continue.

- **0.9** Pass a wooden bridge at left to the Snowmass Center, a **mid-village trailhead** and comfort center. (P)

- **1.0** Stay alert at the Faraway Road intersection.

- **1.2** **Bear left at the sign for the Brush Creek Trail.** (The right fork to Fox Run also connects with the route to Aspen.) Stop at Owl Creek Road after a sharp downhill. Cross, veering slightly left to continue.

- **1.3** **Bear right at the sign for Owl Creek Trail, staying right of the creek.** Cycle past the Snowmass Chapel, Anderson Ranch Arts Center and the Snowmass golf course.

- **1.6** At left is a sign and trail spur for the Snowmass Club where free uphill shuttle rides begin.

- **1.8** Cross Owl Creek Road and ride to its right, passing another sign for Fox Run.

2.3 **Begin biking on Owl Creek Road** at the entrance drive to Two Creeks ski area. You will rejoin the trail at the crest of Sinclair Divide ahead. This section of the journey will be redesigned to better accommodate cyclists. (**P**)

2.4 **Turn right at the intersection** with Highline Road to continue on Owl Creek Road. Begin a big climb.

2.9 **The surface becomes gravel,** making this winding ascent more difficult.

3.2 **At the top of the Divide, bear right at a stone pillar to link up with the paved bike path.** Do not enter the grounds of Mandalay, a vast private estate.

3.3 Cross Owl Creek Road and coast through a pastoral valley, graced by beautiful horses, wide pastures, magnificent homes and an elegantly landscaped red barn.

4.5 A small pond is left of the trail. Ahead are the Woody Creek hills and Red Mountain. A small aspen grove marks a more serious downhill stretch.

5.3 Cycle alongside a working farm. Hay bales are stacked about, and a Victorian farmhouse, unpainted and sagging, decays on the property.

5.6 Begin a steep, winding descent with four hairpin turns. Use brakes carefully. The path meanders away from the road.

5.8 Approach a stop sign at a dirt farm track and begin again to edge Owl Creek Road as it drops gradually alongside airport property.

6.8 **Cross Highway 82 at a dangerous, uncontrolled intersection.** The risk here may vanish if a proposed bike trail is built along the highway's south side. Until that materializes, wait for a big break in the fast-moving traffic.

The trail arcs away from 82 and then parallels the highway, lying between it and the Maroon Creek Club Golf Course.

7.3 The entrance drive to the golf course is 0.2 miles beyond Buttermilk ski area.

7.8 **Pedal over Maroon Creek pedestrian and bicycle bridge** and then beside the Aspen Golf Course, bordered by a rustic fence.

8.6 **Cross Cemetery Lane**, passing tiny Bugsy Barnard Park. **Bear right** onto a bike path that carries you under Highway 82 and toward the Holden-Marolt Mining and Ranching Museum.

Cycle over the Marolt Bridge, which spans Castle Creek.

9.2 Exit the Marolt Trail, turning **left and then right onto Hopkins** Avenue, a designated bikeway. Follow Hopkins to Mill Street.

9.9 Go left one block on Mill to reach Main, the center of Aspen.

> ### Great Little Freebie!
>
> Snowmass Village's extensive paved trail system ties the heights of the Village Mall to the lowlands of the Snowmass Club and golf course. Free town shuttle buses, individually equipped to carry from four to 10 bicycles, load twice hourly at the Snowmass Club shuttle stop, ferrying passengers and their mounts up to the Mall. Cyclists can cruise downhill and hitch a ride back to the heights over and over. Pick up the Brush Creek Trail at the far end of the parking lot opposite Campground Lane and descend, following signs linking the Brush Creek Trail to the Owl Creek Trail to the Snowmass Club. Or just follow your whims to explore the branching trail system.

Snowmass Patios

No cyclist approaching Snowmass Village can dismiss its dramatic and challenging geography. Arrival at the Mall, high in the Brush Creek Valley, justifies, at a minimum, a stop for a tall iced drink. Some visitors lounge at sunny alfresco cafés, enjoying the many free musical performances and festivals that enliven the space. Others seek more elevation, riding the lifts up the ski slopes for some real mountain biking and for a food stop at Dudley's atop Sam's Knob. Restaurants punctuate the Mall area, some conspicuous and others tucked out of sight. Many cyclists dine in the Village before mounting their machines for the mostly downhill spin to Aspen. Bicycles may be rented at numerous Mall locations and mid-village at Snowmass Center.

The Brothers' Grille
5th level of Silvertree Hotel on ski slope

Here's a really out-of-sight restaurant with really nice valley views. Mountain bikers on downhill runs zip past its slopeside patio, but everyone else needs to search it out. One route is up the Silvertree's outdoor steps, where the Mall's concrete meets grass. The Grille's interior has the feel of a ski lodge, but large windows bring the outdoors in. Hikers, equestrians and bikers provide live action for patio diners. This unobtrusive spot features a daily special at a bargain price; a featured dish might be Grilled Meatloaf Sandwich, Tacos, Cobb Salad or Chicken-fried Steak. Call for the current schedule.

Diner Favorites: At breakfast, all Eggs Benedict varieties, Breakfast Parfait, Smoked Salmon Hash. At lunch, Southwest Chicken Sandwich, Caribe Quesadilla, Chicken Caesar Salad.

Summer Hours: Breakfast, 7 am to 11 am; lunch, 11:30 am to 3 pm; dinner, 5 to 10 pm daily.

Etc: Child's menu. Credit cards. Full bar.

Telephone: 923-3520

Grill on the Deck
Mall upper level off Elbert Lane

This lofty perch combines absolutely knockout mountain views with bountiful flowers emblematic of an island paradise. Colorful flora envelopes the deck, spilling from baskets and planters. It is an entirely seductive little hideaway just steps above the Village Mall. Umbrellas in many hues may stand above white tables, but the sun still rules this garden haven. The Grill's light menu items seem right for the café's tropical ambiance. But big appetites may be satisfied too: Meats are smoked on the premises, and the barbecue sauce is homemade. The Grill's indoor partner is the Mountain Dragon, a Chinese dinner restaurant adjacent to the deck.

Diner Favorites: At lunch, Grilled Chicken Breast Sandwich with Jamaican Jerk marinade, Fresh Grilled Ahi Sandwich or Salad, Home-smoked Chicken Salad, two variations of New York Strip Steak Sandwich.

Summer Hours: 11 am to 8 pm daily.

Etc: Credit cards. Happy hour.

Telephone: 923-3576

Paradise Bakery
Mall main level in the Silvertree Hotel plaza

Paradise Bakery in Snowmass Village differs from its Aspen sibling: In place of ice cream and frozen yogurt, it offers sandwiches, soups and salads. And tempting baked goods, naturally. As the indoor counter space is small, carry your chosen goodies outside to a cluster of green tables and chairs, a perfect place to sip cappuccino or read the newspaper. Located near a tall, freestanding clock, this is one of the loveliest corners of the Mall. Trees are encircled by exuberant flowerbeds—masses of paintbox colors. Paradise Bakery is one good excuse to linger here; another is the summer ballet school, whose students practice in an open-air studio just steps from the bakery's door.

Diner Favorites: Chocolate chip cookies, low-fat raspberry muffins, fresh-squeezed lemonade.

Summer Hours: 7 am to 4 pm.

Etc: Cash and checks only.

Telephone: 923-4712

Sage
Snowmass Lodge & Club on golf course

The vista from Sage's two-level patio is big, beautiful, extraordinary. In the foreground, a flower-edged brook burbles into a pond. Lacy aspens and a small footbridge enhance the near scene. Beyond the water stretches the golf course, its undulations meticulously groomed. At a distance, above the ski slopes, stand Mount Daly and Highland Peak, often wearing snowy mantles. Diners linger in this tranquil, elegant scene, luxuriating in the panorama and the food. Cuisine is American with Southwestern accents. Box lunches may be ordered in advance for people on the move.

Diner Favorites: At breakfast, Continental Breakfast Buffet; Three-egg Omelette with Tomato, Basil & Buffalo Mozzarella; Two Eggs Any Style with Herbed Potatoes, Smoked Bacon or Sausage. At lunch, Black Bean Soup, Chilled Seafood Salad, Tortilla Salad, Marinated Grilled Vegetables, Romano Crusted Chicken, all with interesting enhancements.

Summer Hours: Breakfast, 7 am to 11 am; lunch, 11 am to 2:30 pm; dinner, 5 to 10 pm daily.

Etc: Child's menu. Late afternoon light menu. Credit cards. Starbucks coffee. Full bar.

Telephone: 923-0923

S'no Beach Café
Mall upper level

This eatery represents longevity, something reassuring and unusual in resort environments. In the same sunny location since 1976, the S'no Beach deck is positioned perfectly for an above-the-crowd survey of the Mall scene. Savvy locals come early for breakfast: Gone by 10 am is the single pitcher of the fresh-daily Hollandaise for the café's popular Eggs Benedict. For lunch and dinner, Mexican food is well represented, as are soups, sandwiches, salads and burgers. There is a dessert selection and a cappuccino bar.

Diner Favorites: At breakfast, Eggs Benedict variations, Eggs S'no Beach, Huevos Rancheros. At lunch, burgers, including Garden, Beef, Turkey, Chicken Breast, Ahi Tuna; and burritos, including Bean & Cheese, Veggie, Chicken, Beef.

Summer Hours: 7 am to 8 pm daily.

Etc: Child's menu. Credit cards. Full bar.

Telephone: 923-2597

The Stew Pot
Mall main level

Another fixture in Snowmass Village, The Stew Pot has been serving up creative soups and stews and fresh bread since 1972. Sitting smack in the middle of the Mall, alfresco diners often enjoy outdoor entertainment scheduled by the Resort Association. The Stew Pot posts daily specials at its entrance,

but its American menu goes beyond soups, stews and chili to include salads, sandwiches and veggie burgers. The presence of Gatorade says something about this restaurant's broad appeal. In midsummer, you might have to wait for a table. Large planters and green and white umbrellas mark the spot.

Diner Favorites: At lunch, Old Fashioned Beef Stew (yes, even in summer), Fresh Fruit Variety, Summer Sub.

Summer Hours: 11:30 am to 9 pm daily.

Etc: Child's menu. Credit cards. Beer & wine.

Telephone: 923-2263

Wildcat Café
Snowmass Center

Open all year and favored by locals, the Wildcat Café is a mid-village oasis, conveniently close to a post office, bank, grocery store, pharmacy and an Aspen Sports outlet, stocked with bikes for rent. Blessed with an expansive mountain view, the patio is a sunshiny gathering place for Village residents and employees, a spot to observe the day-to-day business of the community. The daily specials are winners here, accounting for half of all sales for lunch and dinner. Breakfast choices should satisfy all tastes and include such items as Smoked Salmon Plate, Veggie Potatoes, and Granola with Bananas.

Diner Favorites: At breakfast, six choices of Fast Breaks, all varieties of Wildcat Benedict, and Breakfast Burritos, which are big all day. At lunch, daily specials, the 6-oz. Fanny Hill Burger, Philly Cheese Steak Sandwich.

Summer Hours: 7:30 am to 9:30 pm.

Etc: Child's menu. Credit cards. Full bar. Takeout.

Telephone: 923-5990

Village Fast Fare

Moon Dogs Cable Car Café
One level below Mall on Daly Lane near shuttle stop

"Moon Dogs," burgers, subs, pizza, popcorn, Italian ices. Breakfast all day. Seating on cable car and at picnic tables. 923-6655

Café Ink!
Mall main level, above D&E snowboard shop

A primo coffee bar! Coffee, hot or ice-blended; espresso shakes, iced chai, fruit smoothies, pastries, bagels, panini. Alfresco or inside. Also on Durant in Aspen. 923-7828.

Goodfellows Pizzeria
Mall upper level

New York style pizza, whole or by the slice; salads, subs. Outdoor stools. 923-2299.

Rocky Mountain Chocolate Factory
Mall main level

Chocolates, other sweets, ice cream, frozen yogurt, coffees, baked goods. Outdoor benches. Also on Cooper in Aspen. 923-2875

Snowmass General Store & Café
Mall upper level

Mexican food, soups, chili, stuffed croissants, pastries. Eat in or takeout. 923-4205.

Snowmass Pizza
Mall main level

Pizza, whole or by the slice; hot dogs, tacos, chili dogs, baked potatoes, subs, salads. Take-and-bake pizza. Outdoor benches. 923-5711.

Village Market
Snowmass Center

Salad bar, hot soups, cool drinks, deli items, fresh bagels and donuts. Takeout. 923-4444.

Bonus

Snowmass Lifts

Imagine gaining easy access to 25 to 30 miles of dirt roads and singletracks snaking across 2500 acres of mountain terrain. The Snowmass ski area delivers multiple routes and panoramic vistas to mountain bikers and hikers via chairlift rides up the slopes. Operating daily in summer, lifts carry cyclists and their vehicles to several launch points. Riding surfaces vary, and bikers should expect dirt, gravel, potholes, rocks and ruts as they thread the narrow singletracks and pedal the ski company maintenance roads. The combination of textured surfaces and steep terrain requires some mountain biking skills and the judicious use of brakes. Beginners should be coached by experienced riders.

The popular program includes operation of the Burlingame and Sam's Knob lifts. Access is on Fanny Hill at the far end of Snowmass Village Mall below the Silvertree Hotel. Lift service may expand. Expect the program to run between early June and early September, weather permitting. Call 925-1220 for specific dates, hours of operation and fee for cyclists over age 12.

From late morning until late afternoon, The Deck at Dudley's at the top of Sam's Knob serves up sandwiches, salads, drinks and snack items. This is dining with a jaw-dropping view. Check it out.

*"A man hath no
better thing under the sun than to eat,
and to drink,
and to be merry."*

—Proverbs, Ecclesiastes 8:15

5 Aspen to Woody Creek

Woody Creek Tavern

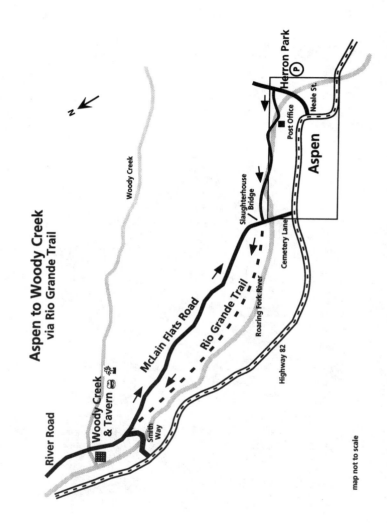

5 ASPEN TO WOODY CREEK
via the Rio Grande Trail

Ride Distance:	16.2 miles round trip from Herron Park
Route Type:	Out-and-back or optional loop
Elevation Change:	480 feet
Riding Surface:	Paved trail, dirt trail, paved road
Terrain:	Nearly flat with one short climb on return to Aspen
Amenities:	Restaurant, water, privy
Highlights:	Riverside route, valley views
Tour Extensions:	Woody Creek to Basalt
	Woody Creek to Lenado

THE RIO GRANDE TRAIL meanders alongside the feisty Roaring Fork River as it traces the old narrow-gauge Denver & Rio Grande railroad bed to Woody Creek. The paved, upvalley portion is frequented by cyclists, runners, walkers and in-line skaters. Stay alert, moderate your speed and warn others if you approach from behind. Private homes overlook the trail and are secreted in trees on the riverbank. Traffic thins out beyond Slaughterhouse Bridge where the unpaved section begins. Houses are replaced by scenic, wild vistas. A **midtown access point** is near the post office on Puppy Smith Street.

While the river's beauty and the exercise are both reasons to saddle up, the real justification for this ride is a hiatus at the venerable Woody Creek Tavern—a singular institution at the heart of an uncommon community.

While riders may backtrack to Aspen, a **recommended alternate return route** follows McLain Flats Road uphill, crosses a bench above the Roaring Fork Valley, and twists downhill to Slaughterhouse Bridge and Cemetery Lane, where it joins the upper Rio Grande. This variation rewards cyclists with killer views.

Access by Bicycle: Begin on Hopkins Avenue one block south of Main (toward Aspen Mountain). Pedal east to Original, which is both an extension of Main and Highway 82. Cross Original carefully and turn left on the street's sidewalk to reach Neale Avenue, a distance of approximately 100 yards. Cycle over No Problem Bridge to the Herron Park trailhead. A midtown trailhead is on Puppy Smith Street; look for a Rio Grande Trail sign just opposite the post office.

Access by Car: In Aspen, drive four blocks east of Mill on Main Street and turn left onto Neale Avenue. Cross No Problem Bridge and park in the designated area adjacent to Herron Park. (P)

0.0 **Start in Herron Park** in east Aspen. The park is equipped with many amenities, including benches and a children's playground. Elevation is 7880 feet. Begin by riding over the first of many bridges spanning the river.

0.2 Cycle by the white tent of Theatre in the Park and the sculpture of the Art Park at right.

0.3 **Bear right downhill**, crossing the Ron Krajian Bridge. Pass the Aspen Art Museum, a brick structure built to house a 19th century hydroelectric plant.

0.4 Pedal underneath Mill Street and over an arched metal bridge.

0.6 **Make a sharp right turn at a Rio Grande trail sign.** This junction near a settling pond and rail fence is the **midtown access point**. Cross two wooden bridges in quick succession.

1.3 At left, a bridge over the river connects to a pedestrian nature path.

1.6 The Picnic Point Bridge leads to both the nature path and a dirt trail to the Aspen Institute campus in the West End. This alternate return route, though short, ends with a sharp climb.

2.2 **Bear left under Slaughterhouse Bridge** to continue to Henry Stein Park and the unpaved leg of the journey. A parking lot across Cemetery Lane makes this yet another trailhead.

ⓟ 🚻 ✖

2.7 Pedal beneath a red, overhanging rock face in this mini-canyon.

2.9 A stagnant pond at right is cluttered with fallen timber.

3.0 Here, opposite Maroon Creek's merger with the Roaring Fork, is access to Stein Bridge. Spanning the river, the bridge links riders to the Airport Business Center and to a bike trail along Highway 82 to Aspen. Now the valley widens, and sun-loving sagebrush replaces trees.

3.8 Pass high above the filtration ponds of Aspen's water treatment plant. In the distance, Mount Daly overlooks the Brush Creek Valley and Snowmass Village.

6.1 A dirt singletrack at left dives downhill to Jaffee Park in Woody Creek. This **optional route** is for experienced riders (or for beginners who dismount). Continue ahead on the wide dirt road for a less bumpy descent.

6.4 **Turn left onto paved McLain Flats Road** and swoop downhill to the intersection of McLain, River Road and Smith Way. Know how to use your brakes. Be advised that intimidating large trucks travel this road.

6.8 **Continue straight ahead at the base of the hill** as McLain Flats melds into River Road. A bike route sign is on the right. This two-lane snakes above the Roaring Fork and below a precipitous hillside. Ride single file as there is no shoulder.

Expect one speed-dip in the road as you approach a mobile home park, the Woody Creek Tavern, a post office and a gallery—the whole of downtown Woody Creek. The defunct Denver & Rio Grande Western Railroad once stopped here to load the cattle of local ranchers.

8.1 **Park your bikes at the Woody Creek Tavern,** a watering hole legendary for a whimsical decor and a clientele of local mavericks. Patrons arrive by bicycle and horse, in pickups and Range Rovers. Bikes may be hub-to-hub out front. Large coolers and a hose supply water for bike bottle refills. Elevation here is 7400 feet.

WOODY CREEK TAVERN

Dedicated to the funky informality of old Aspen and to good eating, the Woody Creek Tavern has bragging rights on lean Limousin beef burgers, Mexican fare and wicked, fresh lime margaritas. If you must wait, camp on a wooden swing outside the log building. A stuffed boar wearing sunglasses perches above the tavern's door, perhaps signaling patrons to drop their cares and their pretensions. Strings of lights shaped like ice cream cones and smiley faces drape from a lattice divider. Secure an outdoor table near an array of giant jars brewing up sun tea. Or venture into the dim, eclectic interior to fuel up before your return trip. Boars' heads project from knotty pine walls plastered with snapshots, posters and old signs. More strands of lights festoon the ceiling: pigs, teapots, Betty Boop, cows, sunflowers, skulls .... The Tavern gives space to a bar, pool table and TVs. Expect full tables and a bustling staff. And have a look at Tavern tee shirts over the bar.

Diner Favorites: Big Limousin Beef Hamburger, Hot Barbecue Pork Sandwich, Fresh Red Snapper Sandwich—all served on onion rolls.

Summer Hours: 11:30 am to 10 pm daily.

Etc: Child's menu. Cash and local checks only. No reservations.

Telephone: 923-4585.

The return ride to Aspen gains 480 feet of elevation, with the most obvious ascent being the short, connecting stretch of McLain Flats Road. Many new cyclists dismount for an uphill walk. To avoid McLain Flats altogether, ride or hike the optional singletrack at the far end of Jaffee Park.

ALTERNATE RETURN
via McLain Flats Road

0.0   **Depart the Tavern and turn right** onto River Road.

1.3   **Ride straight ahead through the intersection** and begin a serpentine climb of 0.7 miles on McLain Flats. Gear down as needed.

1.7   Pass the dirt access road at right to the lower Rio Grande, a turn marked by a white wagon wheel with the red initials "WJ."

2.1   Here, at a second wagon wheel, McLain levels out for a splendid rural ride. As you roll by barns, pastures, hayfields and a few country homes, you enjoy a sterling panorama: Clark Peak, Capitol Peak and Mount Daly are the backdrop to Snowmass Village across the valley; closer to Aspen are the jagged Highlands; Hayden Peak is in the distance. Gently rolling terrain characterizes this bench.

4.0   Trentatz Road at left signals the start of a smooth descent to Aspen. The Airport Business Center is visible on the river's far bank. Red Butte pokes up from the valley floor ahead, and softly contoured Red Mountain is left of the road.

5.2   Sunnyside trailhead is on the left as you sweep downhill.

5.6   **Turn left onto the upper Rio Grande** at Slaughterhouse Bridge to return to midtown Aspen and Herron Park.

To travel over more new territory, continue straight ahead as the road's name changes to Cemetery Lane. Pump uphill for 0.2 miles, pedal by homes and a cemetery, and turn left after one mile onto a bike trail just before an intersection with Highway 82/Main Street. The red, sawtoothed rump of Shadow Mountain is directly ahead. Return to town by trail and West Hopkins Avenue. Signs mark the route.

MILEAGE TIP

Don't dismiss a long bike ride as unrealistic before checking its elevation change and its riding surface. For example, the 30-mile, one-way trip between Aspen and Carbondale is gradually downhill over pavement, except for the four miles of wide dirt trail on the lower Rio Grande. Just start early, drink often and maintain a comfortable pace. The reward is lunch and browsing in Old Town Carbondale before bussing back. Hang your steed on the bus, or, if you have a rental from Ajax Bike in Aspen, drop it off at the Ajax store in Carbondale. Easy.

6 Woody Creek to Lenado

Lenado

Woody Creek to Lenado
via Woody Creek Road

6 WOODY CREEK TO LENADO
via Woody Creek Road

Ride Distance:	21.0 miles round trip from Jaffee Park
Route Type:	Out-and-back
Elevation Change:	1280 feet
Riding Surface:	Paved road, dirt road
Terrain:	Persistent, gradual grade
Amenities:	Restaurant and water in Woody Creek only
Highlights:	Creekside route, unspoiled rural valley
Tour Extensions:	Aspen to Woody Creek
	Woody Creek to Basalt

THIS TOUR THROUGH QUIET COUNTRYSIDE is something of a nostalgia trip: a reminder of life before resort and real estate developers assaulted Colorado's western slope. The Woody Creek valley, with its sheltering hillsides and scarlet soil, is unravished yet: the dominion of cottonwoods, conifers, hayfields, horses, corrals. Old log buildings remain from an earlier time; some decay, empty and silent, while others harbor "Woody Creatures," scrappy citizens dedicated to rural land and lifestyle.

Six miles into the ride, as the road ascends toward Lenado and the Hunter Fryingpan Wilderness, pavement becomes gravel, the valley narrows, and forest supplants farmland.

Access by Bicycle: See Ride #5, Aspen to Woody Creek.

Access by Car: From Mill and Main in Aspen, drive west on Highway 82, passing the turnoff for Snowmass Village at 6.0 miles and turning right onto Smith Way at 6.8 miles. Look for a green sign for Woody Creek Canyon. Smith Way twists downhill, traversing a bridge over the Roaring Fork River at 7.0 miles. To enter the parking area, take a sharp right turn after the bridge at a brown and yellow placard for Wilton Jaffee Sr. Park. (P)

0.0 **Begin at Wilton Jaffee Sr. Park** adjacent to the Roaring Fork River at the intersection of River Rd., McLain Flats Rd. and Smith Way. Trailhead elevation is 7400 feet.

Pedal northwest on upper River Road, paved but minus a shoulder. There is some truck traffic here and little room to maneuver: Ride single file. A green bike route sign and a steep embankment are on the right; the Roaring Fork flows below at left.

Expect two speed dips in the road— one before and one after the **Woody Creek Tavern.**

1.3 **The Tavern,** an uncommon watering hole, lures hordes of cyclists on summer days. For some it is a primary destination; for others, a welcome oasis on the journey to or from Lenado or Basalt.

1.6 **Make a sharp right turn onto paved Woody Creek Road** and pedal a short uphill. The road has no shoulder but is lightly traveled. It quickly flattens out and meanders southeast through pastoral ranchland in a lovely valley watered by Woody Creek.

2.2 Pass Little Woody Creek Road and spans of white fencing. A gentle climb begins.

2.7 Cycle past a road wending uphill to the Aspen Community School, an innovative institution not visible from the bike route.

4.5 Cross a cattle guard, a dip in the road and a second cattle guard as you pedal past the rustic buildings of the Flying

Dog Ranch, home to registered Hereford Limousin cattle, touted as low-fat cows. The road narrows here.

5.2 A cattle guard is accompanied by a yellow sign announcing "Open Range." Be prepared for roaming livestock.

6.3 The road deteriorates to gravel at another cattle guard, marking a turnaround point for riders with lightweight touring bicycles. The valley tightens as the road moves more directly east. Hillsides to the right grow dense stands of tall evergreens, typical of a north-facing slope.

7.5 The elaborate landscaping of Beaver Run Ranch is unexpected in this country environment.

7.9 Vivid red sandstone cliffs overhang the route. This lightly graveled section can be muddy and slippery after a rain. There are many blind corners as this ride advances, and the road drops off precipitously to the creek at right. There are no houses or ranches here.

9.0 You approach a few homes of Lenado's independent residents.

9.6 Woody Creek flows under the road at a concentration of cabins and houses of the Lenado family. Some structures have fallen to pieces, abandoned by the miners and lumbermen who once lived here.

10.0 Pass tailings and more old buildings.

10.1 A Forest Service sign denotes the start of a hiking and mountain biking trail to Aspen by way of Four Corners and Hunter Creek Valley.

10.4 At a second Forest Service sign is the trail register for Woody Creek Trail No. 1994. This footpath enters the Hunter Fryingpan Wilderness and loops back toward Aspen. **No bicycles are permitted in wilderness areas.**

10.5 The turnaround point is a bridge over Woody Creek at 8680 feet of elevation.

6

The downhill return ride rewards cyclists with a splendid mountain panorama of the Maroon Bells-Snowmass Wilderness and with a silky glide on the lower, paved leg. But exercise some caution on the gravel portion: Avoid quick changes of direction and remember to apply more pressure to rear tire brakes to slow your descent.

Lenado's Ghosts

A sense of the past is strong in little Lenado. A few hundred ghosts live side by side with a handful of people who value yesteryear's simplicity. Lenado's boom days in the late 19th century were never glamour days. No brick opera houses or fancy hotels here. This was a utilitarian outpost: log cabins and a boardinghouse; a store, a post office and two saloons; a sawmill, mining sheds, tunnels and a barn for burros and mules. Settlement was prompted by A.J. Varney's discovery of a rich zinc-lead-silver vein in the early 1880s. Men worked two tunnels, the Aspen Contract and the Leadville. The silver panic of 1893 closed the mines and mills. Work revived from 1900 to 1906 but ceased again until 1917 when lead and zinc were needed during World War I. As the demand for strategic metals dwindled, Lenado once more reverted to a ghost town. Life returned in 1935 when Jack Flogaus opened a sawmill to process spruce harvested from Forest Service land on Larkspur Mountain. Those 35 lumberjacks, most only summer residents, have been replaced by a scattering of Aspen dropouts content with the dirt road buffer between themselves and the booming Roaring Fork Valley.

Long ago, an unknown man gave the mining town a Spanish name, pronounced Len-yah-do, meaning "place where wood is cut."

Woody Creek to Basalt

Midland Avenue in Basalt

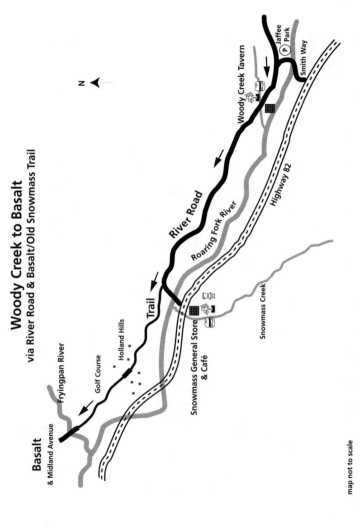

7

WOODY CREEK TO BASALT
via River Road and Basalt/Old Snowmass Trail

Ride Distance:	24.8 miles round trip
Route Type:	Out-and-back
Elevation Change:	776 feet
Riding Surface:	Paved road and paved trail
Terrain:	Rolling with gradual upgrade on return
Amenities:	Cafés, water, restrooms, bike repair, bus service
Highlights:	Riverside route, town of Basalt, restaurant bonanza
Tour Extensions:	Aspen to Woody Creek
	Basalt-Old Snowmass Loop
	Sidetrip to charcoal kilns

THIS PLEASANT RIDE SHADOWS THE ROARING FORK RIVER through a rural landscape overhung by scarlet cliffs and speckled with homes and farm buildings. It attracts cyclists of all abilities. Some favor the gentle downhill glide to Basalt and opt to hang their bikes on an RFTA bus for the uphill return. Others pedal back, needing to burn calories after succumbing to temptation in Basalt's sundry eateries. Everyone enjoys lovely views en route and Basalt's small town character.

The paved road is without a shoulder, but traffic is generally light and cyclists are common travelers. Upper River Road at the ride's start is the busiest section with some trucks and little room to maneuver. Ride single file here and on all winding roads. The paved trail section delights with curves and undulating terrain.

Access by Bicycle: From Puppy Smith Street in midtown Aspen cycle 6.2 miles west on the Rio Grande Trail. See Ride #5.

Access by Car: From Mill and Main in Aspen, drive west on Highway 82, passing the turnoff for Snowmass Village at 6.0 miles and turning right onto Smith Way at 6.8 miles; look for the green sign for Woody Creek Canyon. Smith Way twists downhill, traversing a bridge over the Roaring Fork River at 7.0 miles. To park, make a sharp right turn after the bridge at a brown and yellow placard for Wilton Jaffee Sr. Park. (P)

Jaffee Park, favored by fishermen, is also a launch point for rafting excursions. A good sidetrip is the riverbank foot trail beginning at the far end of the gravel lot.

0.0 **Begin at Wilton Jaffee Park** at River and McLain Flats Roads. Pedal northwest on winding upper River Road, marked by a green bike route sign. The Roaring Fork races along to your left, a partner for the entire ride to Basalt. Trailhead elevation is 7400 feet.

Expect two dips in the road—before and after the Woody Creek Tavern.

1.3 **The Woody Creek Tavern,** a fabled watering hole, lures hordes of bicyclists during summer months. For some it is a primary destination; for others, a diversion on the way to or from Lenado or Basalt. Water is available outside.

1.6 Angling uphill to the right is Woody Creek Road to Lenado. See Ride #6.

2.0 The road bends and crosses the old Denver-Rio Grande Western railroad tracks.

3.5 **Bear right at a fork to continue from upper River Road onto lower River Road.** A sign precedes the split. (The left spur drops downhill to a bridge and Highway 82.) Another bike sign confirms the route. Look for handsome Mount Sopris as you spin downvalley.

4.5 A Burlington Route red caboose decorates the roadside at one of many traverses of the paved-over railroad tracks.

5.5 Wonderful pinnacles and towers of red rock top bluffs rising above spacious pastureland.

7.8 A tiny brick house stands alone on the right.

8.5 **Continue straight ahead to the Basalt/Old Snowmass Trail.** A sign with a map identifies the trail, and arrows point the way.

> The left turn takes you to another bridge over the Roaring Fork; across Highway 82 is the Snowmass General Store and Café.

The trail bends and billows over attractive countryside, moving away from the riverbank. One short, steep uphill requires cyclists to employ good momentum, a low gear or a standing position. A fence edges much of the route, and sagebrush, rabbitbrush and junipers grow nearby. Look for showy dryland flowers in summer.

10.3 **The trail is interrupted** with a ride through the Holland Hills residential subdivision. Brake to make a sharp downhill turn to exit the trail. Bear right and travel several blocks to the street's end. **Turn right and pedal uphill** at a green bike trail sign.

10.9 **Turn left to rejoin the trail** and roll through a golf course and a short, stone tunnel constructed for cyclists. Cross a driveway and pass a tree nursery on your approach to Basalt. A major highway widening project is expected to impact this area in the spring of 1998. Expect a detour followed by a minor realignment of the trail.

11.8 **The bike path ends, connecting with old Highway 82, a two-lane road.** Continue ahead, riding to Cottonwood Drive and then biking across the Fryingpan River bridge to Midland Avenue, Basalt's main street.

12.4 Turn right onto Midland Avenue, an Old West street with wonderful New West restaurants and small shops. At the corner, in Basalt's Lions Park, stands a red caboose, a symbol of Basalt's past as a Colorado Midland Railroad town. Today it houses the Chamber of Commerce office. The old train depot on Midland has been recycled several times, serving now as a bank. Basalt's elevation is 6624 feet.

SIDETRIP

CHARCOAL KILNS

Around 1880, squatters hunkered down at the confluence of two splendid rivers, the Roaring Fork and the Fryingpan. Two years later a tent village and a boardinghouse sheltered men who hewed timber and produced charcoal for smelters in Leadville and Aspen. The charcoal kilns are preserved as monuments to those early workers in this place once named Frying Pan. To see the kilns—remarkable red-rock, beehive-shaped constructions—pedal upriver a few hundred yards on Midland Avenue. Turn right on Riverside Drive, crossing the Fryingpan, and follow Riverside to a bike path that circles the kilns and links Arbaney Park to Basalt's public schools. Cottonwood Drive alongside the school buildings returns you to former Route 82 and the bike trail to back to Old Snowmass and Woody Creek.

After tasting the best of Basalt, cycle back by the same route or hang your bike on a RFTA bus rack for an effortless return. Be advised, however, that there is an extra charge for bikes and competition in midsummer for the four bicycle spaces on each bus.

BASALT'S BEST

On any summer day, as the breakfast-in-Basalt crew pedals back upvalley, it meets the even larger lunch-in-Basalt crowd en route to its own pleasures. And no wonder. The scenery is lovely, Basalt has a laid-back charm, and the cuisine justifies any energy expended. The cafés described were selected for their food and ambiance. But should you not salivate over the choices below, ask around. This small town has other options: Johnny McGuire's no-frills deli, a real Spanish taco stand, a Subway franchise, and The Rotisserie, where fishermen and bikers on the move collect big sandwiches of hot, fresh-roasted chicken.

Café Bernard
200 Midland Ave.

Flower baskets and a few, wee café tables flank the double-door entrance to this tiny gem of a restaurant. With no expansive deck or patio, eating out at Café Bernard could mean eating in. But you will not miss Mother Nature: The intimate indoors has real allure, and the international menu generates an approach-approach conflict. Surrender. You will have no regrets. Inside, flowered tablecloths are topped by glass. The floor is tile, and the windows wear lace. Rosy-peach walls are hung with a changing art exhibit and with co-owner Bernard Moffroid's collection of copper molds and pots. Printed on shirts for sale is the café's maxim: "Where Cowboys Eat Croissants." Breakfast is notable and draws fly fishermen and cyclists, who design their own omelettes or keep it simple with Irish oatmeal made from steel-cut oats. On hot summer days, cool off with iced tea, a delicious secret concoction.

Diner Favorites: At breakfast, Annabelle's Waffles with seasonal fruit, the Morning Bun baked by co-owner Cathy Click, Florentine Omelette with spinach, tomatoes and goat cheese. At lunch, Hot Spinach Salad with pine nuts and smoked turkey, Smoked Turkey & Swiss Sandwich on French baguette or multigrain bread, Caesar Salad with grilled chicken or shrimp.

Summer Hours: T-Sat. breakfast, 7:30 to 11:30 am; lunch, 11:30 am to 2 pm; dinner from 6 pm; Sun. breakfast, 8 am to noon and lunch, noon to 2 pm; closed Sun. nights and Mondays.

Etc: Credit cards. Beer & wine. Reservations requested for dinner.

Telephone: 927-4292

Bistro Basalt
202 Midland Ave.

France melds comfortably into the American West in Basalt. Cooking in the kitchen adjacent to Café Bernard is another French chef, Alain Laval. In contrast to the homey interior next door, Bistro Basalt is sleek and contemporary, all straight lines. But high above the modern paintings and inviting, long granite bar hovers a stamped tin ceiling original to the century-old building. Several umbrella-topped tables edge the front sidewalk, but most alfresco dining takes place on a wonderful, cloistered, two-level deck out back. With a lattice canopy and a fringe of small trees and flowers, the deck is an utterly serene retreat that peeks into the railroad town's past: The funky buildings of Old Town Basalt step up the mountainside from the bistro's backyard. Food at Bistro Basalt is eclectic, international. Late risers can still have breakfast here by indulging in the many egg dishes, all served with Home Potatoes.

Diner Favorites: At lunch, Caesar Salad with chicken, Grilled Chicken Breast Sandwich, the giant 8-oz. Bistro Basalt Burger, Calamari Appetizer with spicy & tartar sauces, Goat Cheese Salad with pasta and walnuts.

Summer Hours: 11 am to 10 pm daily.

Etc: Credit Cards. Full bar. Takeout.

Telephone: 927-2682

Coffee Loft
132 Midland Ave. in Mall, upstairs

Well-named, this pocket-size coffee bar is perched above the street in a sunny corner of the Midland Avenue Mall. The owners, transplants from Hawaii, founded the Smuggler's Brew Coffee Company in the valley and roast their own beans. The Coffee Loft has seating for 16 and shares space with Exposures and Visions, an artist's co-op. A friendly spot, it offers a free paperback book exchange. The Loft sells teas and Hawaiian coffee beans in bags and jars, makes fresh-brewed iced tea daily, and has enticing Lemon Ice Tea Daiquiris on the menu. A small back deck is planned for the Mall's tenants.

Diner Favorites: Frappuccinos, lattes, house Hawaiian coffees, filled croissants.

Summer Hours: 7 am to 7 pm, Sun-W; 7 am to 9 pm, Th-Sat.

Etc: Credit cards. Takeout.

Telephone: 927-1022

Peppercorns Deli & Café
River Park Center, near Texaco and Hwy. 82

A successful Aspen catering business matured into this deli café with New York style. In the sunny space out front, unfancy patio tables are separated from parking by a fence. Inside there is a clean elegance: wood floors and furnishings, cream and deep green walls, brass sconces, framed posters. A blackboard lists daily specials, and shelves display items for sale: vinegars, coffee beans, seasonings, biscotti. A drink cooler should appeal to cyclists, and the pastry case is worth a long look. The deli's patrons, mostly local, have an impressive choice of both hot and cold sandwiches and two or three soups daily in summer. Box lunches should be ordered in advance. At night, Peppercorns serves up sophisticated bistro fare.

Diner Favorites: At lunch, Philly Cheesteak and Grilled Veggie Sandwiches, soups, salads.

Summer Hours: Snacks and lunch, 9 am to 5 pm; dinner, 6 to 10 pm; closed Sundays.

Etc: Credit cards. Full bar. Full takeout menu. Box lunches.

Telephone: 927-4838

Rainbow Grill
181 Basalt Center Circle on the Fryingpan River

When in Basalt, don't miss the Rainbow Grill's deck for a look at the Fryingpan River dashing alongside. Even if you've recently done lunch, you might be tempted to settle in for just a little something more. Maybe one of the 125 domestic, imported and micro-brewery beers from the indoor-outdoor Bear Bar. Maybe a delectable slice of fruit pie from the Grill's own bakery. You get the idea: This is one fantastic location. The Grill's vintage fishing lodge look is absolutely right for this trout mecca. The wait staff wears fishing vests and shorts, the building is crafted from rough wood, stone, old bricks and corrugated tin, and the walls are hung with wildlife aprés taxidermist. (And, yes, that realistic bar bear was once more than a decoration.) Expect a heap of hearty, down-home food here, food meant to satisfy the appetites of hunters and fishermen who home in on Basalt from all over the nation.

Diner Favorites: From the bakery, all pies; at lunch, Chicken-fried Steak, Trout, Ahi Salad.

Summer Hours: Bakery from 8 am daily; lunch from 11 am weekdays; brunch and lunch from 10 am weekends; dinner, 5 to 10 pm.

Etc: Child's menu. Credit cards. Full bar. Takeout.

Telephone: 927-8507

8 Basalt-Old Snowmass Loop

Emma Schoolhouse

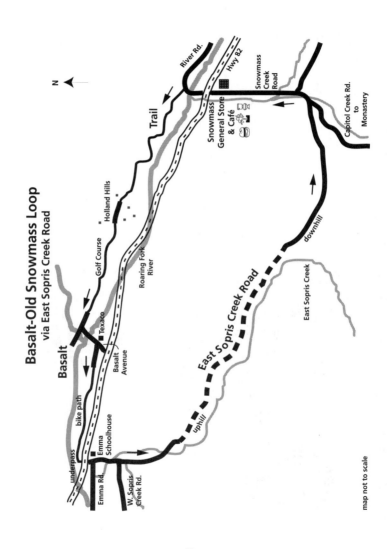

BASALT-OLD SNOWMASS LOOP

via East Sopris Creek Road

Ride Distance:	15.0 miles
Route Type:	Loop
Elevation Change:	826 feet
Riding Surface:	Paved trail, paved road, dirt road
Terrain:	Varied; uphill section before loop midpoint
Amenities:	Café, water, restrooms
Highlights:	Quiet country lanes and magnificent vistas
Tour Extensions:	Woody Creek to Basalt
	Sidetrip to St. Benedict's Monastery

THIS CIRCULAR ROUTE IS AN INTERESTING MIX of engineered trails, rural byways, pastoral ranchland, mountain panoramas and assorted riding surfaces. Full of delightful surprises, the tour is always fresh, never repetitious. It is almost impossible to overstate the natural beauty of the ride. And a sidetrip up Capitol Creek Road to St. Benedict's Monastery might appeal to cyclists eager for more miles and a pervading rural peacefulness.

Basic amenities are found at the Snowmass General Store, 11.2 miles into the trip. But because this loop begins and ends in Basalt, you may visit cafés, rent bikes, acquire accessories or schedule tune-ups before or after your ride. See Ride #7 for a catalog of Basalt's culinary diversions.

Access by Bicycle: Wired for a workout? Ride the 18.6 miles from midtown Aspen to Basalt. See Rides #5 and 7 for details.

Access by Car: From Mill and Main in Aspen, travel 18.2 miles west on Highway 82 to the traffic signal for Basalt. Turn right onto Basalt Avenue. Immediately look for a frontage road on the left, located between 82 and the Roaring Fork River. This is the ride's start and connects to the Emma bike path. Parking options are many. You may drive the first half-mile of the tour and park on the road's gravel edge where the two-lane narrows to a bike trail. *Do not block the nearby private driveway entrance.* But as Basalt is an attractive place with a wealth of amenities, you might motor two blocks to the town center to find free parking on an extension of Midland Avenue, in front of City Hall and the library, and on Two Rivers Road behind the library. (P)

0.0 **Begin on Basalt Avenue** opposite a Texaco station and the shops of River Park Center. Elevation here is 6624 feet. Cycle west on the deadend frontage road past some mobile homes, a few houses, a red barn.

0.5 **Start on the bike path,** parallel to Highway 82.

1.5 Pass a white house and then roll by historic brick structures. Built in 1898 by Charles Mather and preserved today, these western-style commercial buildings served the hamlet of Emma, once a busy railroad stop.

1.7 **Bear left to access a pedestrian/bicycle underpass.** Emerge on the highway's opposite side and ride a few yards to an intersection with signs for both Emma Road and Sopris Creek Road.

1.8 **Turn left toward Sopris Creek Road, passing the white Emma schoolhouse,** a charming relic of the 19th century. The cycling is painless. Level and straight, the road advances to graceful curves through a rural landscape scattered with barns and homes.

3.0 **Turn left onto East Sopris Creek Road at a T-intersection.** This country byway is paved and quiet. It ascends, flattens, then rises and falls. To the right, beyond twisted oak trees, is Mount Sopris, a handsome hill by any standards.

4.3 **The paved surface is replaced by gravel for the next 3.5 miles.** An initial climb of 0.3 miles ends near a beautiful home poised for views. The road and nearby rocks are intensely red. Next, the route undulates over open pastureland before weaving uphill for 0.7 miles. *This is the most taxing portion of the tour—a climb well suited to the low gears of mountain bikes.* Rest and drink liquids if you feel stressed.

6.1 Where the steady incline quits, a splendid vision unfolds: a foreground of hayfields and ranches and a backdrop of snowy sentinels. Standing tall are Capitol Peak, Mount Daly, the Snowmass complex, Highland Peak and neighboring ski runs. It is easy to focus on scenery along this fairly level stretch of road. The **loop's high point** of 7450 feet is reached on this segment.

7.8 **The gravel surface changes to pavement.** Begin a smooth, heady descent. Nearby are some Old Snowmass residences.

8.4 A gold Union Pacific caboose adorns a hillside at left, and the Windstar Foundation, resembling a white bird with outstretched wings, is in the distance.

9.1 **Turn left onto Capitol Creek Road.**

SIDETRIP

St. Benedict's Monastery

If you crave more exercise and more spectacular mountain scenery, turn right onto paved Capitol Creek Road and pedal toward a wall of lofty wilderness peaks and ridges. This sidetrip journeys down a sparsely populated ranching valley to the gates of St. Benedict's Monastery, a serene place in a heavenly setting. The road heaves and dips as it winds gently uphill, gaining 509 feet of elevation on the approach to Monastery Road, 3.1 miles into the ride. A brown sign for St. Benedict's and a left-pointing arrow indicate that the monastery gate is one mile down a gravel lane.

Turn around here, ride farther on Capitol Creek Road or pedal the nearly level gravel mile to St. Benedict's gate.

SIDETRIP, CONT.

> If you have not planned to attend worship services at the monastery's chapel, please respect the monks' silence and separateness by turning back at the gate. An informational sign relates the history of this Cistercian order. St. Benedict's has roots in the sixth century. It supports itself by ranching and by baking Snowmass Monastery Cookies, sold in local markets.

9.4 **Turn left onto Snowmass Creek Road** from Capitol Creek Road. Coast toward Highway 82. There is no shoulder, and a bike route sign advises single-file riding. Traffic, while generally light, is more likely here than on earlier stretches of road.

10.0 Cross a bridge over Snowmass Creek, which now bustles along at left beyond some big cottonwoods. The downhill glide persists.

11.2 **Intersect with Highway 82** at the Snowmass General Store and Café, the Snowmass Post Office and a Conoco gas station—a single, rambling structure that constitutes the hub of Old Snowmass.

> **SNOWMASS GENERAL STORE AND CAFÉ**
>
> A gathering place for local residents, this unpretentious oasis is open most days from 6 am until 9 pm. A water fountain and restrooms are just inside the door; snacks and entire meals are available in the adjacent café. 927-4049.

Cross Highway 82 at a dangerous, uncontrolled intersection and pass over another bridge to continue the circle trip.

11.3 **Turn left onto the Basalt-Old Snowmass Trail** and pedal a short rise to the trailhead. Basalt and the loop's end are 3.7 miles ahead. See Ride #7 for details.

9 Basalt to El Jebel

Bread Aficionado

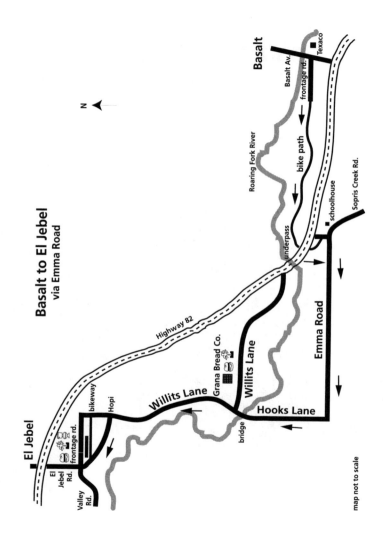

9 BASALT TO EL JEBEL
via Emma Road

Ride Distance:	10.2 miles round trip
Route Type:	Out-and-back
Elevation Change:	146 feet
Riding Surface:	Paved trail and paved road
Terrain:	Flat
Amenities:	Delis, restrooms, bus service
Highlights:	Easy ride, good bread
Tour Extensions:	El Jebel to Carbondale
	Woody Creek to Basalt
	Sidetrip to Grana Bread Company

THIS EFFORTLESS RIDE EXPLORES THE MIDVALLEY REGION by bike trail and country road. Its ease and brevity make it a natural segment of a longer tour. The recommended extension to Carbondale adds miles but requires no additional cycling skills and scant additional effort. El Jebel, once a Colorado Midland Railroad siding, is now a busy and expanding residential and commercial hub. This ride's bakery sidetrip is a must for bread epicureans.

Access by Bicycle: Cycle the 18.6 miles from midtown Aspen to Basalt. See Rides #5 and #7 for details.

Access by Car: See Ride #8.

0.0 **Begin on Basalt Avenue** opposite a Texaco station and the shops of River Park Center. Elevation here is 6624 feet. Cycle west on the deadend frontage road past some mobile homes, a few houses, a red barn.

0.5 **Start on the bike path,** parallel to Highway 82.

1.5 Pass a white house and then roll by historic brick structures. Built in 1898, these western-style commercial buildings served the hamlet of Emma, once a busy railroad stop.

1.7 **Bear left to access a pedestrian/bicycle underpass.** Emerge on the highway's opposite side and ride a few yards to an intersection with signs for both Emma Road and Sopris Creek Road.

1.8 **Turn right onto Emma Road,** a paved and level route through a country scene of pastures, hayfields, horses, barns and a few houses.

> ### Emma
>
> In 1888, at the intersection of a stagecoach road and the newly laid tracks of the Denver & Rio Grande Western Railroad, a small village was built as a rail stop. In naming the place, railroad workers honored Emma Davis Shehi, a rancher's wife and a passionate prohibitionist who often cooked for the men. Evidently, Emma's culinary skills were strong enough to compensate for her condemnation of alcohol. This railroad outpost acquired a schoolhouse, post office, general store, water tank, train station, a few homes, and two commercial buildings embellished with cast-iron columns and fancy brickwork. The white schoolhouse and the brick structures stand today. The post office suspended operations in 1947.

2.9 **Turn right where Emma Road ends** in front of a brick Victorian farmhouse. Cruise downhill on Eagle County Road 8, also named Hooks Lane. Pass cattle, pastures and a several housing developments as you roll toward the Roaring Fork River.

3.5 An exempt D & RG railroad crossing bisects the pavement, and a deadend farm road angles off to the left, parallel to the tracks. Continue on Hooks Lane as it bends sharply right and left before bridging the river. Willits Lane and a tempting, short sidetrip are just ahead.

SIDETRIP

GRANA BREAD COMPANY

The Grana Bread Company is special, worthy of a stop to or from El Jebel. If you crave the best in traditional, handcrafted European breads, wear a commodious daypack to haul home this fragrant, edible art. Approximately six to 10 of the 40-plus bread varieties emerge daily from a French stone hearth oven. Grana Bread Addiction is a highly contagious local affliction. Selection is best early in the day. While five markets in the valley sell some Grana breads, the unique varieties are available only at the source. You may wish to seat yourself inside the bakery, enveloped by ambrosial aromas, to savor scones, biscotti, muffins, soups and sandwiches. Outdoors are two picnic tables set under oaks. Open 7 am to 5 pm weekdays and 8 am to 3 pm Saturdays. No credit cards. 927-1060.

To find the bakery, turn right onto Willits Lane, ride 0.2 miles and turn left into the Midvalley Design Center. The Grana Bread Company is located in the far right corner of the complex in Building 50, Unit 5.

3.6 Turn left onto Willits Lane to continue to El Jebel. Pass open fields and scattered housing. The road angles gently toward the highway.

4.7 Turn left onto Frontage Road before intersecting with Highway 82. This drive leads to Orchard Plaza, anchored by City Market, Alpine Bank and Movieland.

> If you wish to continue to Carbondale and to avoid the busy shopping center, you have two alternatives. Turn left onto Hopi, a residential street in Sopris Village, just before reaching Frontage Road. Cycle west from Hopi to Arapaho. Or turn left just beyond Hopi onto a bike path that passes behind the shopping center's buildings. Both routes will edge a private park and deliver you to the main El Jebel intersection.

4.9 Ride parallel to 82 alongside City Market toward the Movieland theaters.

5.1 **The El Jebel intersection** at Valley Road is this ride's western terminus. An underpass connects to a Wendy's franchise, a bowling alley, a bus stop and El Jebel Plaza, home to several fine dinner restaurants. Elevation here is 6480 feet.

El Jebel Portable Edibles

Bagel Bites
near City Market, 963-9169

Big menu with bagel-everything, novel cream cheese spreads, fruit smoothies galore, espresso drinks, Bud's Mud homemade ice cream. Limited seating.

Capitol Deli
near Movieland, 963-4333

Winning sandwiches: Hot Chicken, Grilled Veggie, and Gyros, "made the real Chicago way." Cold bottled drinks, salads, brownies. Seating inside & out. Closed Sundays.

City Market
Orchard Plaza, 963-3360

Deli, fresh produce, bakery, sport bars, cold drinks.

Formula Uno Bakery
near Movieland, 963-2284

Foccacia and its kin—panini & pizza. Calzone, Italian salads, fruit spritzers. Deck seating. Closed Sundays.

Wendy's
at the Texaco Station across Hwy. 82, 963-9813

10 El Jebel to Carbondale

Catherine Store

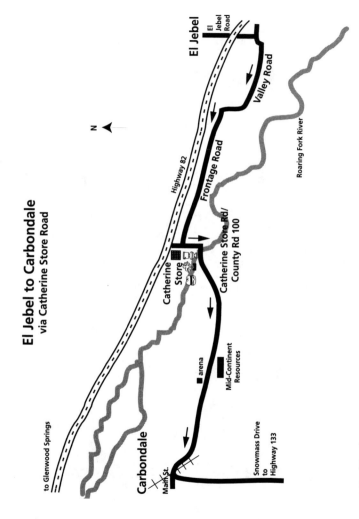

10 EL JEBEL TO CARBONDALE
via Catherine Store Road

Ride Distance:	14.4 miles round trip
Route Type:	Out-and-back
Elevation Change:	299 feet
Riding Surface:	Paved roads
Terrain:	Flat
Amenities:	Cafés, water, restrooms, bike repair, bus service
Highlights:	Catherine Store, Old Town Carbondale
Tour Extension:	Basalt to El Jebel

CARBONDALE HAS REAL COLORADO CHARACTER, an understated charm, and a tempting roster of unique shops and alfresco eateries. This small town, with its own big mountain, draws repeat visitors. But the relaxed, friendly nature of Carbondale has also lured new residents, some from nearby Aspen and others from distant California and Latin America. These transplants add spice to a mix of ranchers and farmers, artists and artisans. Carbondale's summer Mountain Fair and autumn Potato Days are celebratory traditions born in different eras of different cultures, but both reflect an adaptable, inclusive spirit.

Pedal through horse country over the level valley floor for an easy, rural ride. Quirky little Catherine is a distinctive midpoint oasis and marks the place where almost nonexistent auto traffic increases to light traffic. Expect warm temperatures and intense sunshine in summer.

Access by Bicycle: Start in Aspen for a 24-mile warm-up.

Access by Car: Follow Highway 82 northwest from Aspen. At the El Jebel traffic signal, 4.1 miles beyond the Basalt intersection, turn left. The bike tour begins here. Park your vehicle in the Orchard Plaza shopping complex, left of the turnoff. Biking from Basalt through Emma adds 10 easy miles to the round trip. (P)

0.0 **Begin at the main El Jebel intersection** just west of the shopping area anchored by City Market. Across Highway 82 is a Texaco station, Wendy's and a cluster of good restaurants. Elevation here is 6480 feet.

Follow Valley Road, a quiet lane bordered at left by farmland and hillsides. This level ride to Catherine threads the space between the Roaring Fork River, secreted in trees beyond the fields, and Highway 82. Mount Sopris towers above nearby ridges.

1.1 Valley Road curves right, toward 82.

1.3 **Turn left onto Frontage Road** just before reaching 82. Parallel the highway on this wide, flat surface.

2.4 Flying Fish Road disappears into trees by the river.

3.7 **Turn left onto Catherine Store Road** from Frontage Road at the curious and inviting junction known as Catherine. Elevation is 6284 feet.

CATHERINE

Now only a crossroads, Catherine was never more than a collection of ranches, a post office managed by ranch wife Catherine Staufacher, and a place where the Colorado Midland train slowed down for a tossed exchange of mailbags. The "depot" was a solitary train car. The Silver Crash of 1893 was nearly fatal to the valley's economy; eventually the railroad pulled out and the post office closed. But around 1930, Herman Hoaglund built a store just west of the post office site, erecting it on stilts because of swampy ground. Later a drainage ditch was dug, and in 1958 Charles Harris replaced the original structure with the present building. Harris had the ultimate general store, stocking a gigantic supply of Levi's jeans and selling groceries, gas, hardware, beer and, sometimes, snowmobiles and motorcycles.

Catherine Store today wears a delightfully eccentric façade concocted by the Lael Hughes family during its tenure: The rambling old building is adorned with a painted mural and is encircled by giant, carved, wooden figures of bears, cowpokes and Indians and by relics of 19th century wagons. Giving more homage to the past are the brightly painted wall representing an imagined main street, complete with railroad tracks down its center, and prominent signs for the fictional "Blacksmith and Livery Stables" and "Saloon." A wooden horse's head protrudes through a false stable window, and a carved cowboy squats inside the rickety outhouse in back.

The present is delineated by working gas pumps, a real liquor store and the Catherine Store itself, with its unlikely mix of antiques, new country crafts, potato chips, mounted elk heads, a big wooden Santa, a producing grapefruit tree, newspapers, bogus boxes of "Roadkill Helper," ice, chilled waters, teas and sports drinks. An outdoor hose near the store's east corner supplies fresh well water for drinking or cooling off. A restroom is inside. Open 6 am to 10 pm weekdays and 7 am to 8 pm on Sundays. 963-2156.

Expect light traffic as you pedal this narrow, undulating country road, the back route to Carbondale. There is no shoulder; for safety, ride single file.

4.3 Cross a bridge over the Roaring Fork River just before the road curves to the right. Farms, hayfields and horses are very much in evidence and represent continuity with the work of the area's first white settlers.

5.9 At left are buildings of Mid-Continent Resources, a closed coal mining operation. Carbondale's economy, initially agricultural, grew rapidly after coal deposits were discovered nearby. But in the early 20th century, the need for coal as fuel was affected when the smelting and silver mining industries declined. Mid-Continent hung on for several decades before shutting its doors.

6.0 A white, fenced, dirt arena is on the right.

7.2 **Cross railroad tracks into Carbondale** at a bend in the road. Ride quaint Main Street past inviting shops and restaurants, a vintage movie theater and U.S. Forest Service headquarters. More entrepreneurs, antique dealers and decorators flourish on side avenues. Sidewalk benches are the dominion of old-timers in overalls and tractor caps, puzzling, no doubt, over peculiar visitors sporting aerodynamic head gear and body-hugging lycra. A few blocks down Main at 7th Street is Sopris Park, equipped with a drinking fountain, picnic tables, shelters and public restrooms.

Main Street extends to Highway 133, where new expansion is evident. The town's elevation is 6181 feet, while Mount Sopris, its handsome, granite neighbor, sports twin peaks of 12,953 feet.

Snack Tip

Even if you plan a café lunch, a snack in your bike bag or pocket is insurance against flagging energy. Just a bite or two can fuel you for a few extra miles. Studies show that cyclists who add some carbohydrates during a trip can pedal an hour or more longer than companions who consume nothing. Packaged low-fat energy bars and gels are easy to tote along. If a ride is longer than three hours with no stops for food, pack something substantial, such as a bagel or a sandwich. And consider bananas. They have a good carbohydrate-calorie ratio plus potassium, which fights cramps by moving lactic acid out of active muscle tissue.

Carbondale Cuisine

Cruising for cuisine in Carbondale means savoring the flavors of Main Street: It's all cooking right there. Stroll the avenue, chew on tasty possibilities, graze or feast, and then sample the diverse fare in local shops. Within steps of each other are an upscale art gallery, transplanted from Aspen, and a crammed resale shop, claiming to be the "best in the West." You may wish for more time to nibble on Carbondale. All the eateries profiled below have outdoor tables for the fresh-air crowd, but there are other choices: Peppino's doles out New York pizza; the Old Nugget offers affordable pub grub inside a brewery; Clark's Market deli constructs popular turkey breast, veggie and hummus sandwiches; and Il Pazzaluna Ristorante serves up sophisticated Italian food in a beautiful, cool space.

Desert Sky Restaurant & Bar
801 Main Court

This restaurant may turn its face away from Main Street, but the big white house with its colorful flags and visible deck welcomes all who favor foods of the Southwest. Umbrellas shade alfresco diners who may choose from imaginative soups, such as Tortilla or Yellow Squash, and a range of pasta dishes, traditional Mexican favorites and Southwestern fare. Navajo Taco Salad comes in many variations, and burgers go by colorful names: Coyote, Rattlesnake, Santa Fe. Desert Sky often replaces beef with lean buffalo meat.

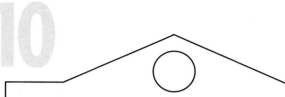

Diner Favorites: At lunch, Western Caesar Salad with chicken, salmon or shrimp; all Enchiladas; the daily special of pasta and a salad.

Summer Hours: Lunch, 11:30 am to 5 pm; dinner, 5 to 10 pm; Sunday brunch, from 10 am.

Etc: Credit cards. Child's menu. Takeout. Happy hour, 4 to 6:30 pm.

Telephone: 963-1306

Java Joe's Coffee Bar & Eatery
433 Main St.

Friendly and inviting, this coffeehouse is a place to mingle, to relax and to inhale the heady aroma of fresh-roasted coffee. In the historic building's linear space, a brick wall exhibits art for sale. Small tables hug the wall, each set with fresh flowers. A back room, painted red, holds comfy furniture, a bookshelf, magazines. Two tables occupy a sunny spot outside the front door. Expect to find a variety of pastries and coffee specialties plus deli sandwiches and salads. Smoothies and Ben & Jerry's are right for summer, as are the frozen novelty items and cold drinks in freestanding cases. Java Joe's also brews up coffee in downtown Basalt.

Diner Favorites: Don Corleone sandwich, Berry Plunge smoothie, latte and mocha latte.

Summer Hours: 6:30 am to 10 pm, M-F; 7 am to 10 pm, Sat., Sun.

Etc: Cash and local checks only.

Telephone: 963-0573

Landmark Restaurant & Bar
689 Main St.

Both a restaurant and a bed-and-breakfast inn, the Landmark boasts two separate outdoor spaces. Breakfast is served on the east deck, where the morning sun counters cool temperatures.

By midday, diners are more comfortable on the westside patio, tucked under shade trees and umbrellas and treated to a view of Mount Sopris. The menu is American with a tilt toward the Southwest. Lunch items range from Popeye Salad—spinach with orange vinaigrette—to Chicken-Fried Steak and the Pot Pie of the Day.

Diner Favorites: At breakfast, Huevos Landmark with pork green chili; French Toast with fresh fruit; River Mist—shrimp & crab folded into hash browns, topped with cheese and eggs; Hawg Wild—ham, onions & mushrooms combined with potatoes, cheese & eggs. At lunch, Cobb Salad; Classic Caesar Salad with chicken, salmon, crab or shrimp; Honey Mustard Chicken Sandwich.

Summer Hours: 7:30 am to 10 pm daily; weekend breakfast available until 3 pm.

Etc: Credit cards. Child's menu. B & B. Full Bar.

Telephone: 963-1850

Ship of Fools Restaurant & Bar
348 Main St.

Carbondale's semiarid natural environment is a long reach from the sea, but no matter. Ship of Fools compensates with a seaside decor and fresh fish entrées. Lunch salads may be ordered with chicken or tuna. Locals favor the stew and two soups cooked up each day. Veggie pizza suits other customers. Fish is largely served at dinner, and the menu always includes shrimp scampi, swordfish, salmon and catfish. Look for a brick building wearing green paint and a tall fence enclosing a spacious patio. Carbondale's only open-pit barbecue is positioned at the patio's far end. Bordered by trees, this outdoor room comfortably holds a dozen round tables, log benches and even bicycles. The restaurant provides water and an air pump to needy cyclists.

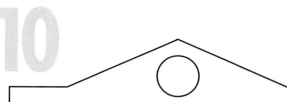

Diner Favorites: At lunch, Albacore Tuna Sandwich, Fish-on-a-Roll, Bonedale Veggie Sandwich, Ship's "Titanic" 8-oz. burger.

Summer Hours: 11 am to 10 pm daily (for food). Dinner from 5 pm.

Etc: Credit cards. Child's menu. Full bar.

Telephone: 963-3606

The Village Smithy Restaurant
Main St. at Third St.

This red structure, with horseshoes and anvils near its door, was once a working blacksmith's shop. Recycled as a breakfast and lunch restaurant, it bustles all summer. Inside, an assortment of old wooden chairs, walls of brick and pine, and a changing exhibit of local art impart a comfortable feel. Outside, an awning-shaded terrace steps down to a patio and wide lawn. Contemporary marble sculpture coexists with old wagon wheels and farm implements. Myriad menu items include Smithy "Lite Fare" for healthy eating. Chilled soups are among the summer specials. The weekend lunch menu is abbreviated so that patrons may indulge in breakfast all day. Baked items, including huge cookies, are homemade. Indecisive diners may struggle with the array of choices. The Smithy is entirely nonsmoking and sells some jams, oils, coffees, pottery and cards.

Diner Favorites: At breakfast, Huevos Rancheros; McGurk's—hash browns with veggies & cheese; and McHuevos, a combination of the two favorites above, served on a flour tortilla. At lunch on weekdays, all South-of-the-Border Specials, Chicken Fajitas, Sandy's Turkey Delight Salad, Oriental Salad, and the locals' choice—Sparky's Hot Chicken Salad.

Summer Hours: 7 am to 2 pm daily.

Etc: Credit cards. Extensive child's menu. Senior citizen discount. Takeout drinks and baked goods.

Telephone: 963-9990

11 Basalt-Carbondale Loop

Mount Sopris

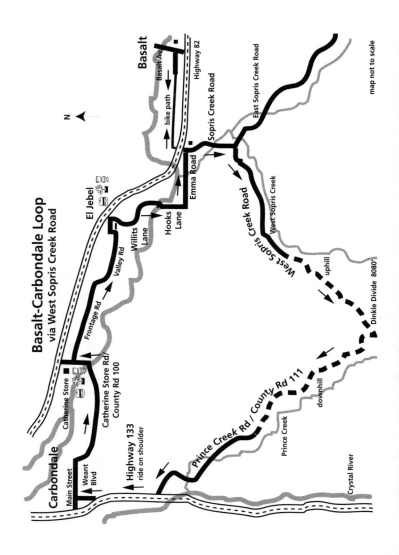

11 BASALT-CARBONDALE LOOP

via West Sopris Creek Road

Ride Distance:	29.0 miles
Route Type:	Loop
Elevation Change:	1899 feet
Riding Surface:	Paved trail, paved road, dirt road
Terrain:	Mixed; a steady climb to 8.7-mile point
Amenities:	Cafés, water, bike repair, bus service, restrooms
Highlights:	Back roads, big views, Carbondale
Tour Extension:	Woody Creek to Basalt

THIS LOOP IS THE BOOK'S MOST AMBITIOUS TOUR—an elevation gain of 1456 feet in the first 8.7 miles, some rough surfaces and substantial total mileage. The route has a bit of everything: vast cattle ranches, proximity to Mount Sopris, lonely BLM land, Old Town Carbondale and a strip mall. The first amenities are found 16 miles into the journey.

Because a stretch of this loop is uninhabited and lightly traveled, one rider in the group should carry a spare tube and tools. Everyone should have ample water and a rain shell. Mountain bike front shocks, while not necessary, are a plus on the downhill gravel portion of Prince Creek Road.

Access by Bicycle: Fired up? Ride the 18.6 miles from midtown Aspen to Basalt. See Rides #5 and #7 for details.

Access by Car: See Ride #8.

11

0.0 **Begin on Basalt Avenue** opposite a Texaco station and the shops of River Park Center. Elevation here is 6624 feet. Cycle west on the deadend frontage road past some mobile homes, a few houses, a red barn.

0.5 **Start on the bike path**, parallel to Highway 82.

1.5 Roll by historic brick structures. These western-style commercial buildings served the hamlet of Emma, once a busy railroad stop.

1.7 **Bear left to access a pedestrian/bicycle underpass.** Emerge on the highway's opposite side and ride a few yards to an intersection with signs for both Emma Road and Sopris Creek Road.

1.8 **Turn left toward Sopris Creek Road passing the white Emma schoolhouse,** a charming relic of the 19th century. Level and straight, the road advances to graceful curves through a rural landscape scattered with barns and homes. Capitol Peak and Mount Sopris appear and disappear from the horizon.

3.0 **Turn right on West Sopris Creek Road at a T-intersection** and begin a sharp climb of 0.3 miles over a paved surface. The ascent moderates at a scattering of homes, horses, corrals and rustic fences. After a mile, all buildings vanish. This is empty, arid country.

4.9 Cross the first of four cattle guards as you ride directly toward massive Mount Sopris.

5.6 **The road surface changes to dirt** as it continues to ascend. It is generally well maintained. The valley widens here.

6.6 Sopris Mountain Ranch, tidy and attractive with its red barns, red house and broad pastures, is at left. The giant mountain itself is the main view ahead. The scenery is worth a long look.

8.3 **Turn right at a brown and yellow sign for Dinkle Lake and begin a steep uphill,** biking away from Mount Sopris.

8.6 The road makes a big U-turn toward the mountain.

8.7 **Continue ahead,** passing the dirt lane at left leading to Dinkle Lake and the Mount Sopris trailhead. This is the Dinkle Divide and the loop's high point of 8080 feet. **Begin a long descent to Carbondale over a dirt and gravel surface** known as Prince Creek Road. You have an aerial view of the town.

8.9 Cross a cattle guard at an old corral. The road curls through an unpeopled landscape.

9.5 A Bureau of Land Management sign announces, "Entering Public Lands."

10.0 A recreational trailhead for the Prince Creek corridor is at left. The BLM has developed access points to about 20 miles of dirt roads and singletracks beginning just east of Dinkle Divide. Maps are available from the BLM in Glenwood Springs.

10.9 A sign notes, "Leaving Public Lands," and another reads, "Crossing private land. Please stay on road. Respect landowner's rights."

12.1 Pavement replaces gravel, and a brown house signals a return to civilization. The twisting road is made for cruising.

13.3 Much of Carbondale comes into sight at a red barn where the road bends right.

13.7 Enter Garfield County where Prince Creek Road is identified as County Road 111. Homes are widely spaced here.

14.1 The road slips through a notch cut in a small ridge.

14.9 Turn right onto Highway 133 at a stop sign. *Ride the paved shoulder on this busy route.*

15.4 A Carbondale city limit sign states the town's elevation of 6181 feet.

> At 15.8 miles, Snowmass Drive to the right bypasses Old Town Carbondale to connect directly to Catherine Store Road for the first leg of the return trip. Ride 0.6 miles to a railroad crossing and intersection with Catherine Store Road.

16.0 Turn right onto Weant Boulevard for the Carbondale Central Business District. On the corner is a log cabin with dormers, relocated to the spot and preserved as the Carbondale Mount Sopris Historical Museum. Built in 1882, it is known as the Holland-Thompson cabin. Cycle past a school and Sopris Park.

16.4 Go right on Main Street to find abundant restaurants, intriguing shops and a comfortable ambiance. Take a break in Old Town Carbondale. It's a charmer. See Ride #10 for details.

16.7 Cross railroad tracks and continue the loop by traveling Catherine Store Road through a country scene.

19.6 Cross a bridge over the Roaring Fork where the road bends.

20.2 **Turn right onto Frontage Road at Catherine Store,** an eclectic, well-appointed comfort stop. Ride parallel to Highway 82 on this flat, wide surface.

22.6 **Turn right onto Valley Road,** a semirural lane. The cycling is easy.

23.9 Continue through the El Jebel intersection, passing the Orchard Plaza shopping center.

24.3 **Turn right onto Willits Lane.**

25.4 **Turn right onto Hooks Lane** (Eagle County Road 8), cross the Roaring Fork again, and pedal a gradual uphill.

26.1 **Curve left onto Emma Road** where Hooks ends.

27.2 **Bear left at the intersection where Emma Road becomes Sopris Creek Road. Head toward 82 to find the highway underpass.** Cycle the bike path back to Basalt.

29.0 **The loop ride ends in Basalt.**

12 Glenwood Canyon

Glenwood Canyon

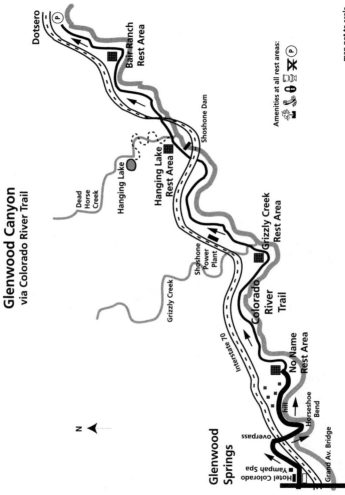

12 GLENWOOD CANYON
via Colorado River Trail

Ride Distance:	25.8 miles round trip from No Name; 30.8 from town
Route Type:	Out-and-back
Elevation Change:	300 feet from No Name; 354 from town
Riding Surface:	Paved trail
Terrain:	Gentle grade with undulations
Amenities:	Water, restrooms, picnic tables
Highlights:	Dazzling river canyon scenery
Tour Extension:	Hike option to Hanging Lake

THE NATURAL DRAMA OF GLENWOOD CANYON cannot be exaggerated. The Colorado River, alternately wild and placid, and the soaring fiery cliffs, built of horizontal bands of rock, make this a stunning place. When an intensely blue sky pairs with the canyon's brilliant reds and greens, it is a scene not be missed. A concrete bicycle path traces the river's curves, sometimes only a few feet from the water. Kayaks and rafts lurch and bob in the river, and an occasional train plys the tracks on the far bank. Rest areas are thoughtfully spaced to provide amenities, wondrous views and picnic sites. While a slight downslope makes for an easy return, headwinds are common here, so expect to do a little pedaling.

Cyclists share the popular river trail with walkers, runners and in-line skaters; stay alert! As the Glenwood area can be quite warm at midday in midsummer, schedule a ride based on your tolerance for heat. Should you opt for the sidetrip hike to Hanging Lake, bring locks to secure your bicycles at the trailhead. **And remember that any rest area on the route can serve as a trailhead.** Recreational traffic is light on the east, upper end of the canyon path.

Access by Bicycle: Drive, or ride a RFTA bus, to Glenwood Springs. Bicycles may be rented at shops on Grand Avenue, 7th Street or at the Hotel Colorado across from the Hot Springs Pool. Begin on 6th Street at the hotel and cycle past the Yampah Spa and Vapor Caves as you ride parallel to Interstate-70. A bike and pedestrian bridge carries you safely over the busy highway. Follow unused, old Highway 6 & 24 past the Horseshoe Bend picnic area. Use lower gears to pedal a hill to the tiny community of No Name where you pick up the paved Colorado River Trail. **The No Name trailhead is 2.5 miles from town.**

Access by Car: From Aspen, drive 40 miles northwest on Highway 82 to Glenwood Springs, where 82 is named Grand Avenue. If you carry your bikes on your automobile, cross the Grand Avenue bridge over the Colorado River, pass the Hot Springs Pool, park on 6th Street and follow the directions above; if starting in town, add 5.0 round trip miles to the tour. Or bear left over the bridge, following signs for Interstate-70 east to Denver. Drive to Exit 119 for No Name—2.5 miles from the bridge in Glenwood Springs. Exit and turn left at the stop sign to reach the parking lot. (P)

0.0 **Begin at the No Name trailhead. Water, restrooms, bike racks, telephones and parking are available here and at all rest areas along the route.** Follow bike trail signs downhill to the riverbank. The I-70 highway is to your left, shielded from view for much of the trip. Elevation at riverside is 5800 feet.

1.7 A stone pillar supports a sign reading "Entering White River National Forest."

2.5 **The Grizzly Creek Rest Area** has outdoor seating and shade trees. Rafts and kayaks put in here to ride Class I and II rapids. Cross a small bridge over Grizzly Creek to continue.

4.5 The Shoshone Hydroelectric Plant has been generating electricity since 1909 and today supplies power to Denver residents. Many rafts and kayaks launch here to catch the excitement of Class III and IV rapids.

5.8 Cliffs on the river's far side mimic the turrets and towers of a fortress. An occasional Amtrak train rumbles over the tracks, continuing the canyon travel that began in 1887 when wealthy tourists departed Denver for Glenwood's Spa in the Rockies.

6.6 As you cycle under the highway, rapids are before you; and when snow is still melting in the high country, water plummets from the rock face at left.

6.9 The river drops over the Shoshone Dam spillway, and I-70, temporarily to your right, emerges from a tunnel in the canyon wall.

7.2 **The Hanging Lake Rest Area**, beautifully situated, also serves as a gateway for the climb to Hanging Lake. The river is subdued and glassy here, tamed by the dam downstream. It reflects florid pinnacles, towers and forts of sedimentary rock laid down in colorful bands. The highway's tunnels preserve tranquillity.

7.6 **Hanging Lake Trailhead** is just short of a bridge spanning Dead Horse Creek, outflow from the lake above. Picnic tables and an antique wagon perch on the riverbank. For a great combination outing, secure your bikes here to climb the 1.2 miles to lovely Hanging Lake. Every hiker should carry water and should drink every 15 to 20 minutes.

SIDETRIP

HANGING LAKE HIKE

This scenic sidetrip should be taken seriously: The steep path is a jumble of rocks and sandy soil; it gains 1060 feet of elevation as it switchbacks north/northwest up a gulch, crossing Dead Horse Creek on footbridges again and again. The creek plunges downhill, rich with melodic waterfalls. Sun and shade alternate as the trail twists beneath trees and giant red cliffs. Simple log benches and a tiny shelter are comforts, touches of civilization on the way to a Arcadian scene—a scene best savored in the early morning when birds outnumber humans.

SIDETRIP, CONT.

At the turn of the century, visitors rode flat rail cars to the trailhead. Glenwood Springs maintained the land as a public park for nearly 50 years. A restaurant, stable and resort complex once stood near the river, and guides led horseback riders to the lake. An informative placard near the trailhead explains the lake's origins, ecology and fragility. Please respect this vulnerable natural wonder.

Signs along the climb direct hikers to both Hanging Lake and to Dead Horse Creek trail, a separate excursion. Near the lake, just beyond stairsteps in a cliff, is a spur trail to Spouting Rock, a recommended mini-sidetrip. Here an underground stream spurts from a limestone face, and a cascade drops from a cleft in a towering wall. Together they spawn a shower, a cooling mist and a fine photo opportunity.

Hanging Lake is a tiny aquamarine gem fed by lacy waterfalls and adorned with emerald mosses. A wooden boardwalk safeguards the lake's periphery—a delicate layer of dissolved minerals deposited by the water. Miniature islands, anchored to fallen timber, sprout wildflowers and grasses. Brook trout frolic, their lives preserved by a ban on fishing. Wordsworth could have found inspiration here.

10.3 A sign on highway above reads "Leaving White River National Forest."

10.7 **The Bair Ranch Rest Area** is the final oasis on the upriver trip. It is named for the Bair family's sheep ranch, and it features a riverside hiking loop and a launch point for flatwater canoes.

12.4 An Eagle County sign and an expanding horizon mark the terminus of Glenwood Canyon.

12.9 **The Colorado River Trail ends** near Dotsero, the ride's east portal. Elevation here is 6100 feet. (P)

13 Glenwood to Fish Hatchery

Hotel Colorado

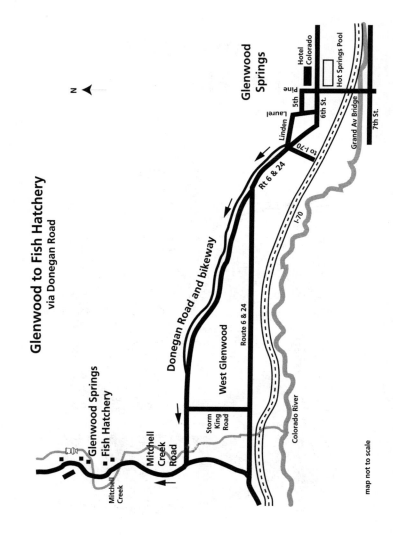

13 GLENWOOD TO FISH HATCHERY
via Donegan Road

Ride Distance:	8.0 miles round trip
Route Type:	Out-and-back
Elevation Change:	374 feet
Riding Surface:	Paved trail and paved road
Terrain:	Rolling with one long hill
Amenities:	Restroom at hatchery
Highlight:	Tour of trout-rearing facility

THIS LITTLE RIDE EXPLORES WEST GLENWOOD and delivers cyclists to the State Trout Hatchery and Rearing Unit, beautifully situated on the flanks of Storm King Mountain. Take a self-guided tour to learn about the fingerling and broodstock programs at the hatchery; visit raceways and nurse basins to view kokanee salmon and several species of trout; and enjoy the experience of feeding these beautiful fish.

The cycling is easy except for the final hilly mile up Mitchell Creek Road to the hatchery. Try out your low gears and take your time. Imagine the heady descent and think about the rewards that await you on your return to town: delectable pastries, fruit smoothies, aromatic coffees, hearty bagels . . . . But remember that two of Glenwood's great bakery cafés close by early afternoon.

Access from Aspen: Ride an RFTA bus or drive 40 miles northwest on Highway 82 to Glenwood Springs, where 82 is named Grand Avenue. Bicycles may be rented at shops on Grand and on 7th Street and at the Hotel Colorado. If you carry your bikes on your automobile, cross the Grand Avenue bridge over the Colorado River, pass the Hot Springs Pool, park on 6th Street and begin the ride. (P)

- 0.0 **Begin at the far end of the Grand Avenue Bridge over the Colorado River** where 6th Street passes between the Hot Springs Pool and the Hotel Colorado. Elevation here is 5746 feet. Ride uphill on Pine, passing the front entrance to the historic hotel. **Turn left on 5th Street** at the Pizza Hut **and right on Laurel Street** at 0.2 miles; Laurel becomes Linden Street before it delivers cyclists to the beginning of the bike trail to West Glenwood.

> To sample a fine breakfast or to indulge in opulent pastries before a morning excursion, ride the sidewalk for a few blocks on 6th street (Route 6 & 24) toward West Glenwood and look for Rosi's Little Bavarian Restaurant on the right just past the turnoff for Interstate 70. The Glenwood Motor Inn nearly surrounds the small structure. Continue on the same sidewalk to connect with the bike trail.

- 0.4 **Pick up the bike trail to the right of** Route 6 & 24. The Colorado River is far below the road at left.

- 1.1 **Turn right onto Donegan Road at a fork,** pedal a short uphill, and travel the road or the concrete sidewalk/bikeway. The terrain is gently rolling. Donegan, also called County Road 130, parallels 6 & 24 but is primarily a residential street above the traffic and commercial buildings.

- 1.5 Continue on Donegan past Sunny Acres Road, an uphill spur to the Glenwood Springs public golf course.

- 2.3 The sidewalk/bikeway ends near a school. Charred, standing timber on a hilltop ahead marks the eastern terminus of the 1994 Storm King Mountain fire. Fourteen fire fighters died in that lethal blaze.

2.7   Pass Storm King Road and then cross a small bridge spanning Mitchell Creek. Reposition your bike's gears for an extended climb.

3.0   **Turn right onto Mitchell Creek Road** and begin a significant one-mile uphill. Gear down as needed and breathe deeply. This narrow country lane has no shoulder, but it is quiet and is certainly the prettiest part of the ride. Along the road are Gambel oaks, horses, a few log homes and the handsome wooden fence of Storm King Ranch. The creek, which has been out of view at right, twice passes under the road as you approach the destination.

4.0   **Enter the fish hatchery grounds.** A sign welcomes you to the State Trout Hatchery and Rearing Unit at Glenwood Springs, a facility of the Colorado Division of Wildlife. While five species of trout are raised here, one important focus is to nurture and reintroduce the threatened A+ strain of Colorado River Cutthroat Trout, the only trout native to local alpine lakes and streams. The hatchery also produces all of the state's Lake/Mackinaw Trout.

The hatchery's setting is quite wonderful. Since 1905 its buildings have occupied a narrow slash in the mountain, sharing the vertical space with Mitchell Creek. Fish swim in open tanks and pools. A self-guided, interpretive walk includes visits to 10 numbered stations. Peer through windows in the main hatchery wall at one stop on this outdoor circle tour. For 25 cents visitors may buy food to feed the fish.

Restrooms are open Monday through Friday only. Visitors may bike or hike uphill on a gravel road for an additional mile. Elevation at the hatchery is 6120 feet.

Glenwood Fare

Unlike upstart Aspen, Glenwood has always been something of a resort: In its prehistory, long before European-Americans built a spa here, the Ute Indians frequented the area's hot mineral springs, often camping for the winter season. For many travelers, a mention of Glenwood Springs elicits images of both a stately hotel with Italian ancestry and a colossal pool with steam lifting from its thermal waters. But for others, a reverie of Glenwood conjures up forms of profligate pastries and redolent breads, served up by their creators. To them, Glenwood is a bakery town. Five of the establishments profiled here are proper bakeries—whatever their monikers, whatever the breadth of their menus. Most occupy buildings within Glenwood's historic core. A stroll will uncover other choices, such as Chevy's 57 on 8th, which resembles a 1950s-style soda fountain, and Quizno's on Grand, which serves up subs and salads.

Bagel Bites
725 Grand Ave.

Aspen's successful bakery café spawned this Glenwood outlet. The space is wonderful: a lofty ceiling, a wood floor and a huge barnlike door set into one of its brick walls. Tables cluster in the front windows and step down the restaurant's length. Bagel addicts find everything here: bagels unadorned; bagels smeared with exotic cream cheeses; bagels stuffed with salmon or eggs or hummus; bagels stacked high with sundry sandwich fixings.

Smoothie enthusiasts discover smoothie heaven, where the vast array includes Rice Milk Splash, a nondairy option. And ice cream fans dip into Bud's Mud, the café's homemade handiwork. A different sort of customer was served here in the 19th century when the space housed a saloon.

Diner Favorites: Turkado Sandwich, Aspen Veggie Sandwich, Mud Pie High double espresso-ice cream drink.

Summer Hours: M-Sat., 7 am to 7 pm; Sun., 8 am to 6 pm.

Etc: Cash and local checks only. Takeout.

Telephone: 928-8804

Calder's Market Coffee & Tea Company
8th St. & Grand Ave. near bridge

Coffee and tea aficionados have a haven in Glenwood. This roasterie serves up fine coffee concoctions, scones, beignets, biscotti, breads, sandwiches and a bargain-priced pizza-and-salad combo. For sale are bulk coffees and teas, mugs and teapots. Inside are a polished wood floor and light, pickled, wood walls topped by a dark band of plum, floral wallpaper. Tables by the front window look out onto the café's alfresco diners and the busy street scene. A large table occupies the center space, and more seating is back by the roasting room. Two Hungarian armoires impart a homey, living-room feeling. Both elegant and comfortable, this is a place to tarry. The Calder's Market site was once the posh Hotel Glenwood where outlaw Doc Holliday lived after the OK Corral gunfight. Holliday, suffering from tuberculosis, died at the hotel in 1887.

Diner Favorites: White Mocha Latte, Spinach & Feta Croissant, Cinnamon Beignet, green tea, coffee.

Summer Hours: Sun.-Th, 7 am to 10 pm; F, Sat., 7 am to 11 pm.

Etc: Credit cards. Takeout.

Telephone: 945-2055

Courtyard Café at Hotel Colorado
6th St. & Pine St.

While only steps from the ado of the hot springs pool and the Grand Avenue bridge, the Courtyard Café seems a separate world—screened from the bustle by leafy trees, old-fashioned hollyhocks, and the soothing splashes of a fountain. It is a flowery garden scene planted at the base of a replica of the Medici Palace. Fashioned in the 16th-century Italian style, the Hotel Colorado was designed by New York architects Boring, Tilton & Mellon and built in 1893 by Aspen "Silver King" Walter Devereux. Wander its ground floor hallway where hang photographs of notable patrons: Presidents William Taft and Theodore Roosevelt, actor Tom Mix, gangsters Al Capone and Diamond Jack Alterie, philosopher-psychologist William James and others. The café's lunch menu features sandwiches, burgers, pastas and salads—such as Smoked Trout Salad with field greens and pecan lime vinaigrette. The Champagne Sunday Brunch offers up varied entrées: Duck Spinach Salad, Seafood or Wildberry Crêpes, Grand Marnier French Toast.

Diner Favorites: At lunch, all salads with a glass of wine; at Sunday brunch, Champagne and Salmon Croissant Scramble with capers & cream cheese.

Summer Hours: M-Sat. breakfast, 7 to 11 am; Sun. breakfast, 7 to 10 am; Sun. brunch, 11 am to 2 pm; lunch, 11:30 am to 2:30 pm; dinner, 6 to 10 pm.

Etc: Credit cards. Child's portions. Full bar.

Telephone: 945-6511

Daily Bread Café & Bakery
729 Grand Ave.

Glenwood locals sigh with relief when tourists depart at summer's end: They can reclaim the Daily Bread, a Grand Avenue fixture and purveyor of enticing baked goods and meals, both immoderate and fat-free. Enter and confront a pastry case laden with pleasures such as flaky apple strudel, Grand Marnier Mousse Cake and divine chocolate chip cookies big enough for lunch. Fancy coffees to accompany fancy pastries include the Snickers, a caramel and chocolate latte. Diners also confront a broad menu that should leave no one unsatisfied. Bread choices for toast or sandwiches are extensive, and the low-fat/fat-free items, introduced in 1995, now account for half of all summer orders. Stained glass, plants and lace curtains trim the front windows. Wood tables and booths hold customers, and walls dressed in pine paneling and wallpaper exhibit art for sale. A tiny back dining room wears soft pastels. In the 19th century, this building functioned as a restaurant, a saloon and a drugstore.

Diner Favorites: From regular breakfast menu, Cinnamon Roll French Toast, Greek Omelette, Breakfast Burrito, Huevos Extraordinaire; from regular lunch menu, Grand Avenue Deli Sandwich, Chicken Caesar Salad, and Bacon, Turkey & Avocado on sourdough. From low-fat breakfast menu, Fat-free Granola, Egg White Scramble with veggies, and omelettes adapted from regular menu; from low-fat lunch menu, Chicken Caesar Salad and Tuna Niçoise Salad.

Summer Hours: M-F, 7 am to 2 pm; Sat., 8 am to 2 pm; Sun., 8 am to noon, breakfast only.

Etc: Credit cards. Child's menu. Takeout from bakery. Senior citizen discount.

Telephone: 945-6253

Rosi's Little Bavarian Restaurant & Pastry Shop
141 W. 6th St. at Glenwood Motor Inn

To really appreciate Rosi's, enter without inhibitions. For just a while, permit yourself to be a hedonist. Jettison guilt and contemplate the delicacies in the pastry case. Then be seduced by the best of Bavaria. Whether you are here for the gossamer Heavenly Torte, White Chocolate or Ricotta Cheesecake, Mint or Mocha Torte, granola, a Danish or a full breakfast, be assured that everything is homemade—even jam, salsa, and almond filling for strudel. The restaurant's bright new sunroom is seductive too. The Bavarian theme is interpreted in fresh blue and white and pine. A lace valence crowns the windows, and twig wreaths adorn the walls. The ceiling is angled for a cozy effect. Owner-chef Rosi Huff now cooks dinner and, while her focus is German food, she prepares a daily American special and Prime Rib every Saturday. To find Rosi's, pedal or walk a short distance west of the Grand Avenue bridge and the turnoff for I-70. On the right, nearly encircled by the Glenwood Motor Inn, is a wee building painted with a wall mural of German children and the Bavarian Alps.

Diner Favorites: From the pastry case, Rum Torte, Black Forest Cake, Fresh Fruit Flan, Apple Torte, Sacher Torte, Cherry Crumb Cake, Napoleons; at breakfast, Eggs Benedict, Eggs Neptune, Veggie Benedict, Biscuits & Gravy, pancakes, waffles; add mimosas on the weekends.

Summer Hours: M-Sat. breakfast, 7 am to noon; Sun. breakfast, 7 am to 1 pm. Dinner W-Sat., 5 to 10 pm. No lunch.

Etc: Credit cards. Full bar. Takeout.

Telephone: 928-9186

Wild Rose Bakery
310 7th St. near bridge and train station

One-half block west of Glenwood's historic train station is this tiny bakery café. Housed in a low brick building in what was once the town's seedy red light district, it looks directly across the river at the imposing Hotel Colorado. Above the door a colorful oval sign illustrates a muffin, a mug and some wild roses. Two sidewalk tables flank the entrance, and four round tables set with fresh flowers rest on a polished wood floor inside. Walls are sponged with peach paint and hung with quilts for sale. The old tin ceiling is white. It is a bright, light, clean space. Wood cupboards hold a water cooler, teas and hot water, and a microwave for warming pastries. Cases display the three or four breads of the day, cakes, pies, muffins and other sweet goodies. Lunch items include foccacia variations, Spinach-Ricotta Turnovers, Mozzarella-stuffed Herbal Rolls and a daily soup. The owners use organic ingredients for baking and make their summer salads from organic greens. Fancy coffee drinks are good partners for the pastries. The bakery's name honors the co-owner's favorite Alaskan flower.

Diner Favorites: Raspberry Cream Cheese Crumb Cake, Sour Cream Coffee Cake, Fruit Danish, both oatmeal and chocolate chip cookies.

Summer Hours: M-F, 7 am to 5:30 pm; Sat., 7 am to 5 pm; Sun., 8 am to 3 pm.

Etc: Credit cards. Takeout.

Telephone: 928-8973

"Without bread, without wine, love is nothing."
—French proverb

THE AUTHOR

RUTH FREDERICKS FREY acquired her fondness for Rocky Mountain trails in the mid-1970s and now makes her summer home in the Aspen area. With her husband Peter, she wrote *The Aspen Dayhiker*, a guide to wilderness trails, introduced by Brush Creek Books in 1993. Two years later she completed *Aspen On Foot*, a book of shorter hikes, nature trails, local history and fishing.

THE ARTIST

DONNA CURRIER is a freelance illustrator who began her professional career in Denver where she designed advertisements, worked as a courtroom artist and created graphics for television. Now in the Midwest, she applies her skills to a wide range of projects. Donna illustrated both *The Aspen Dayhiker* and *Aspen On Foot*.

REFERENCES

Alley, Jean, and Hartley Alley. *Colorado Cycling Guide*. Boulder: Pruett Publishing Company, 1990.

Bancroft, Caroline. *Unique Ghost Towns and Mountain Spots*. Boulder: Johnson Publishing Company, 1967.

Barlow-Perez, Sally. *A History of Aspen*. Aspen: WHO Press, 1991.

Dallas, Sandra. *Colorado Ghost Towns and Mining Camps*. Norman: University of Oklahoma Press, 1985.

Dowling, Mark. *Bike with a View: Colorado's Front Range and Central Mountains*. Denver: Concepts in Writing, 1994.

Nealy, William. *Mountain Bike! A Manual of Beginning to Advanced Technique*. Birmingham: Menasha Ridge Press, 1992.

Olofson, Jack O., ed. *The Best of Colorado's Biking Trails*. Denver: Outdoor Books and Maps, Inc., 1994.

Pearce, Sarah J., and Roxanne Eflin. *Aspen and the Roaring Fork Valley*. Evergreen, Colorado: Cordillera Press, Inc., 1990.

Pearson, Mark L. *Run, Bike, Blade: A Local's Guide to Fun in Aspen*. Aspen: M&L Graphics, 1994.

Rossetter, Laura. *Mountain Biking Colorado's Historic Mining Districts*. Golden, Colorado: Fulcrum Publishing, 1991.

Stoehr, William L. *Mountain Bike Rides in the Colorado Front Range*. Boulder: Pruett Publishing Company, 1988.

Stuart, Robin, and Cathy Jensen. *Mountain Biking for Women*. Waverly, New York: Acorn Publishing, 1994.

Summary Data for the Rides[*]

Ride #	Route Name	Miles	Elevation Change	Riding Surface	Midpoint Restaurant
1	Aspen West End Tour	4.8+	190	paved/dirt	Yes
9	Basalt to El Jebel	10.2	145	paved	Yes
10	El Jebel to Carbondale	14.4	300	paved	Yes
12	Glenwood Canyon	30.8	300	paved	No
13	Glenwood to Fish Hatchery	8.0	375	paved	No
5	Aspen to Woody Creek	16.2	480	paved/dirt	Yes
4	Snowmass Village to Aspen	19.8	695	paved/dirt	Yes
7	Woody Creek to Basalt	24.8	775	paved	Yes
8	Basalt-Old Snowmass Loop	15.0	825	paved/dirt	Yes
2	Aspen to Ashcroft	21.2	1500	paved	Yes
6	Woody Creek to Lenado	21.0	1280	paved/dirt	No
3	Aspen to Maroon Bells	21.2	1640	paved	No
11	Basalt-Carbondale Loop	29.0	1900	paved/dirt	Yes

[*] Rides listed in approximate ascending order of difficulty. Mileage is for round trip distance.

Café Cycling Ride Summaries

Notations for Rides 1, 2 and 3 assume a start from midtown Aspen. Other points may also serve as trailheads for these tours.

Aspen West End Tour
and Golf Course Loop

0.0	Mill & Hopkins in Aspen. Ride west on Hopkins to 7th.
0.7	Left on 7th to Marolt Trail and Bridge. Right toward Cemetery Ln.
1.0	Right under Hwy. 82.
1.2	Cross Cemetery Ln. Left to circle Aspen Golf Course.
2.0	Straight to continue loop. Pass homes fronting golf course
2.9	Left and downhill on Cemetery Ln.
3.4	Right onto Rio Grande Trail.
4.0	Right at Picnic Point Bridge. Left fork and uphill to Institute.
4.3	Meadows Restaurant.
4.4	Left on North from bikeway. Left on 5th to Music Tent.
4.8	Music Tent, Harris Concert Hall. Exploration of West End streets. Historical Society on Bleeker.

2 ASPEN TO ASHCROFT
via Castle Creek Road

- 0.0 Mill & Hopkins in Aspen.
       Ride west on Hopkins to 7th.
- 0.7 Left on 7th to Marolt Trail and Bridge.
       Left at sign for Castle Creek Rd.
       Pass Museum and Marolt housing.
- 1.0 Left on Castle Creek Rd. near hospital.
- 11.6 Ashcroft townsite.
- 13.0 Pine Creek Cookhouse.

3 ASPEN TO MAROON BELLS
via Maroon Creek Road

- 0.0 Mill & Hopkins in Aspen.
       Ride west on Hopkins to 7th.
- 0.7 Left on 7th to Marolt Trail and Bridge.
       Right toward Cemetery Ln.
       Left at sign for Maroon Creek.
       Cross Castle Creek Rd.
       Continue on trail, passing chapel.
- 1.8 Aspen schools campus.
       Begin riding Maroon Creek Rd.
- 2.9 Highlands Ski Area.
- 4.8 T-Lazy-7 Ranch.
- 6.3 Forest Service station.
- 10.6 Maroon Bells area.

4 SNOWMASS VILLAGE TO ASPEN
via Owl Creek Trail

- 0.0   Campground Ln. below Mall.
        Bike to far end of adjacent parking lot.
        Ride Brush Creek Trail.
- 1.2   Left at sign for Brush Creek Trail.
- 1.3   Right at sign for Owl Creek Trail.
- 2.3   Ride Owl Creek Rd.
- 2.4   Right at intersection. Hill climb.
- 2.9   Road surface becomes gravel.
- 3.2   Rejoin paved Owl Creek Trail.
- 6.8   Cross busy Hwy. 82.
- 7.8   Maroon Creek Bridge.
- 8.6   Cross Cemetery Ln. Bear right under highway.
        Cross Marolt Bridge.
- 9.2   Left from trail to Hopkins Av.
- 9.9   Aspen's center.

5 ASPEN TO WOODY CREEK
via Rio Grande Trail

- 0.0   Herron Park in east Aspen.
- 0.3   Right and downhill to Krajian Bridge.
- 0.6   Right at sign. Midtown access point.
- 2.2   Left under Slaughterhouse Bridge.
        Trail surface becomes dirt.
- 6.4   Left and downhill on McLain Flats Rd.
- 6.8   Straight ahead on River Rd.
- 8.1   Woody Creek Tavern.

Alternate Return

- 1.7   Continue uphill on McLain Flats Rd.
- 5.6   Left onto paved Rio Grande.

6. WOODY CREEK TO LENADO
via Woody Creek Road

- 0.0 Jaffee Park at River & McLain Flats Rds.
       Ride northwest on River Rd.
- 1.3 Woody Creek Tavern and post office.
- 1.6 Right onto Woody Creek Rd.
- 6.3 Riding surface becomes gravel.
- 9.6 Lenado.
- 10.5 Turnaround at bridge over creek.

7. WOODY CREEK TO BASALT
via River Road & Basalt/Old Snowmass Trail

- 0.0 Jaffee Park at River & McLain Flats Rds.
       Ride northwest on upper River Rd.
- 3.5 Right at fork onto lower River Rd.
- 8.5 Straight to connect to bike trail.
- 10.3 Holland Hills trail interruption.
- 10.9 Rejoin trail.
       Roaring Fork Club golf course.
- 11.8 Straight on old Hwy. 82.
- 12.4 Midland Av. in Basalt.

8 BASALT-OLD SNOWMASS LOOP
via East Sopris Creek Road

0.0 Basalt Av. opposite Texaco.
     Ride west, parallel to Hwy. 82.
0.5 Emma Bike Trail.
1.7 Left to highway underpass and intersection.
1.8 Left toward Sopris Creek Rd., passing schoolhouse.
3.0 Left onto East Sopris Creek Rd. at T-intersection.
4.3 Road surface becomes gravel. Begin climb.
7.8 Road surface becomes pavement. Descend.
9.1 Left onto Capitol Creek Rd.
9.4 Left onto Snowmass Creek Rd.
11.2 Cross busy Hwy. 82.
11.3 Left onto Basalt-Old Snowmass Trail.
12.9 Holland Hills trail interruption.
13.5 Rejoin trail.
     Roaring Fork Club golf course.
14.4 Straight on old Hwy. 82.
15.0 Midland Av. in Basalt.

9 BASALT TO EL JEBEL
via Emma Road

- 0.0 Basalt Av. opposite Texaco.
  Ride west, parallel to Hwy. 82.
- 0.5 Emma Bike Trail.
- 1.7 Left to highway underpass and intersection.
- 1.8 Right onto Emma Rd.
- 2.9 Right onto Hooks Ln. at Victorian farmhouse.
- 3.6 Left onto Willits Ln.
- 4.7 Left into shopping plaza. Continue straight.
- 5.1 El Jebel Rd. & Valley Rd. intersection.

10 EL JEBEL TO CARBONDALE
via Catherine Store Road

- 0.0 Valley & El Jebel Rds. west of shopping plaza.
  Follow Valley Rd.
- 1.3 Left onto Frontage Rd., parallel to Hwy. 82.
- 3.7 Left onto Catherine Store Rd. at store.
- 4.3 Bridge over Roaring Fork River.
- 7.2 RR tracks & Old Town Carbondale.

11 BASALT-CARBONDALE LOOP
via West Sopris Creek Road

0.0 Basalt Av. opposite Texaco.
Ride west, parallel to Hwy. 82.
0.5 Emma Bike Trail.
1.7 Left to highway underpass and intersection.
1.8 Left toward Sopris Creek Rd., passing schoolhouse.
3.0 Right onto West Sopris Creek Rd. at T-intersection.
5.6 Road surface becomes dirt.
8.3 Right and uphill at sign for Dinkle Lake.
8.7 Straight ahead at Dinkle Divide high point.
Downhill on Prince Creek Rd.
12.1 Road surface becomes pavement.
14.9 Right onto shoulder of Hwy. 133.
16.0 Right onto Weant Blvd. at log cabin museum.
16.4 Right onto Main St. in Carbondale.
16.7 RR tracks.
Straight on Catherine Store Rd.
20.2 Right onto Frontage Rd. at store.
22.6 Right onto Valley Rd.
Straight at El Jebel intersection.
24.3 Right onto Willits Lane.
25.4 Right onto Hooks Lane.
26.1 Left onto Emma Rd. at Victorian farmhouse.
27.2 Left at intersection with Sopris Creek Rd.
Highway underpass to bike trail.
29.0 Basalt.

12 GLENWOOD CANYON
via Colorado River Trail

0.0	6th St. near Hotel Colorado. Ride east passing Vapor Caves. Cross bridge over I-70. Pedal uphill to No Name.
2.5	No Name trailhead and rest area.
5.0	Grizzly Creek rest area.
9.7	Hanging Lake rest area.
10.1	Hanging Lake hike trailhead.
13.2	Bair Ranch rest area.
15.4	End of canyon bike path.

13 GLENWOOD TO FISH HATCHERY
via Donegan Road

0.0	Hotel Colorado, 6th St. & Pine. Uphill on Pine. Left on 5th. Right on Laurel. Left on Linden.
0.4	Bike trail parallel to Route 6 & 24.
1.1	Right on Donegan Rd. at fork.
3.0	Right and uphill on Mitchell Creek Rd.
4.0	Fish hatchery grounds.